HISTORIC UNDERGROUND MISSOULA

NIKKI M. MANNING

Foreword by Dr. Kelly J. Dixon

THE History PRESS

Published by The History Press
Charleston, SC 29403
www.historypress.net

Front cover: Front Street looking west, circa 1900. *Library of Congress, LC-USZ62-116750*; basement room in Missoula Mercantile, 2013. *Photo by Bethany Hauer.*
Back cover: Archaeological surface collection, Missoula Mercantile basement, 2013. *Photo by Nikki Manning*; tunnel inside the Missoula Mercantile basement, 2013. *Photo by Kelli Casias.*

First published 2015

Manufactured in the United States

ISBN 978.1.62619.919.4

Library of Congress Control Number: 2014959297

To my grandmother, Thelma Irene Strogish, for being the first person to say that if archaeology is what I wanted to do, I should throw away the doubts and go do it.

CONTENTS

Contents

FOREWORD

One of my feet gripped the bottom rung of the ladder while the other touched down on the damp, uneven, mucky earth. The air in the subbasement was dank, and I could hear droplets of water falling from somewhere. I could not see a thing in the darkness except for the beam of light coming from the crawl space cut into the basement floor above. I reached up above my forehead to switch on my headlamp and examined another one of Missoula's enigmatic underground spaces as part of the Missoula Historic Underground Project. The owner of this particular building was leading our archaeology class through a labyrinth of subterranean features that served multiple needs for the building's tenants, as well as for the structural integrity of the building itself. For safety protocol, I was bringing up the rear and within communication distance of a responsible graduate student, Nikki Manning, who remained at the opening of the crawl space above for the moment.

Looking around the subbasement, I could see beams of light bobbing ahead in the darkness, as the archaeology students' headlamps lit up rubble foundation remnants that had been in place for over a century and concrete walls strong enough to hold back a river. The students' voices expressed something between exhilaration and the thrill of exploration—I felt myself caught up in the adventure of being able to learn something about human use of underground spaces. "What a priceless opportunity for University of Montana (UM) students," I exclaimed up to Manning. Manning agreed, descended the ladder and was inspired, during the course of our fall 2012 archaeological survey class, to take on Missoula's historic underground as her MA thesis project, the outcome of which represented the first definitive overview of the Missoula underground and which is the topic of this book.

Ms. Manning's project, like many, began as a conversation with one of the local cultural preservation specialists. In this case, I visited with the now retired Missoula historic preservation officer, Philip Maechling, and we discussed the importance of developing an underground history project in 2005. The first UM student who worked closely with Missoula's Historic Preservation Office (HPO) to help unravel the mysteries and urban legends associated with Missoula's underground architectural and archaeological features was Laura Chase. Chase started the initial phase of this project during an internship with the HPO in the spring of 2005. The project proved to be larger and more complicated than anyone expected, requiring multiple teams working in archives and in "the field" (downtown Missoula), and it took time to develop the right mix of preparation and opportunity for the project to take off.

In 2012, the Missoula HPO reached out again, and that was when the multiyear project began with students (about fifty total) enrolled in UM archaeological field methods courses. Participants learned how to conduct a mix of archival investigations, oral histories, artifact analyses and systematic inventories and documentation of Missoula's underground spaces. The goal of the 2012 and 2013 archaeological survey classes and the 2013 Urban Archaeological Field School, and one of the pressing goals of Manning's thesis research, was to provide Mr. Maechling with some fact-based answers to the community's questions about Missoula's underground cultural heritage. In the process, we began to question our own biases and some of the powerful narratives that thrive via Missoula's local collective memory. A few years later, the Missoula Historic Underground Project generated evidence about this underground landscape that is presented by Manning in this book. Everyone involved in the underground investigations in downtown Missoula became aware of how urban archaeology has a role in urban planning, historic preservation decision making and in understanding the importance of adaptive reuse during a time when we are attuned to sustainable and practical ways of managing urban ecosystems.

The Missoula Historic Underground Project integrated research and education, with Missoula's underground spaces and historic landscapes becoming learning labs where students participated in a "real-world" project dedicated to documenting and investigating the archaeological and architectural remains of Missoula, Montana's downtown National Register of Historic Places district and amid the context of urban planning. Students learned techniques of urban archaeological survey, historic building documentation and analysis, test excavations, oral and historical source interpretation and public relations amid a bustling downtown area. The field courses emphasized skills intended to prepare students for futures where they will be expected to provide archaeological and historic preservation–based input on planning and decision making in settings with historic urban landscapes.

Many of these landscapes, including places like the Missoula Downtown Historic District, hold deep meaning for the local and transnational communities connected to this city's historic places and spaces. Missoula's underground landscape has fueled a wave of public engagement with University of Montana and local HPO events. We marveled at the turnout of people associated with underground tours and information-sharing meetings regarding the progress and findings of the Missoula Historic Underground Project. We realized early that there was something about the underground itself that seemed to captivate people. Whether stories of clandestine uses of urban undergrounds during the U.S. era of alcohol prohibition or reports of tunnels running beneath a street to connect a bank, a mercantile and a hotel, every person who learned about this project was instantly enchanted and expressed interest in learning the outcomes of our urban archaeological investigations taking place literally right beneath where people stood on the sidewalk in downtown Missoula.

Since time immemorial, humans have built and used subterranean structures. Underground urban spaces are ubiquitous throughout the world, with below-ground areas providing spaces for food and drink storage, living, transit, commerce and mausoleums, to name some of the most common uses. Here, Nikki Manning presents Missoula, Montana's underground story, underscoring the fascination and contributions of narratives of local project participants and providing a systematic, fact-based report on the underground features. In the process, Manning demonstrates how this story of Missoula's historic underground cultivates an appreciation for cultural resource and preservation laws.

This project teaches us to behold with an archaeological eye and to garner an appreciation for underground cultural features as living parts of the community and as worthy of preservation via adaptive reuse, particularly in light of the loss of information about underground spaces often being overlooked by traditional historic surveys. Indeed, the story of Missoula's historic underground changed the way I look at Missoula's urban landscape. I will not likely see the downtown area quite "normally" ever again.

DR. KELLY J. DIXON
Professor
Department of Anthropology
University of Montana
Missoula, Montana
kelly.dixon@mso.umt.edu

PREFACE

In the late summer of 2012, the now retired Missoula historic preservation officer Philip Maechling approached Professor Kelly Dixon at the University of Montana with a request to help him answer some questions about the city's underground landscape. Many people asked him over the years whether he knew anything about Missoula having a historic underground like other towns in Montana, including Havre and Butte, both of which have lucrative historical underground tours that run year-round. There are other cities across the American West that have popular undergrounds as well, with three of the most popular being Portland, Oregon; Seattle, Washington; and Sacramento, California. Mr. Maechling asked Dr. Dixon if she and/or a few students might be interested in following up on some research he and another UM student, Laura Chase, had begun several years earlier so that he would have at least a few facts he could share with the inquiring public who wanted to know the truths behind the local lore of Missoula's underground.

That autumn semester, Dr. Dixon discussed this potential project of exploring Missoula's underground with the archaeological survey methods class, and all the students were enthusiastic about the possibilities of "going underground" in historic downtown Missoula. Although it was a place full of mystique and folklore that many had heard about (but had not seen), local collective memory included many opinions about the city's underground history. Thus began the Missoula Historic Underground Project—a project I do not think any of us anticipated would become so vast. This project is laced with enough historical, architectural and archaeological data and potential data to fuel many theses, dissertations and books for years to come.

Questions about the underground have been asked by residents and tourists alike in Missoula over the years. You can strike up a conversation with just about any person on the street or sitting at a local bar or restaurant and they will probably have a story to tell, either from personal experience or something told to them by someone who knew someone who has "been in the tunnels." Conversations with business owners in downtown Missoula about the topic almost inevitably end with a question of whether I would like to see their basement and a unique feature of some kind.

Some of the folkloric memories that have been told over the years are that the tunnels under Missoula were built by the Chinese in the late nineteenth or early twentieth century. The Chinese, it is often said, used the tunnels and underground spaces as opium dens and for moving about the city undetected during a time when being Chinese in the Unites States and particularly in the American West was quite difficult and even dangerous. Stories also suggested that sometimes gentlemen used the tunnels to access the female boardinghouses (brothels) without being seen and others for running illegal alcohol products during the Prohibition era.[1]

It is not out of the question that Missoula would have an underground. Just 120 miles to the southeast is Butte with a rather extensive underground, and Havre, 280 miles to the northeast, also has a famed underground. Add to the list popular underground sites in Boise, Portland, Pendleton, Sacramento and Seattle, and it is understandable that people would assume the same would exist in Missoula. Indeed, Missoula has some of the same features as these other places—tunnels, basements with perplexing features and spatial voids under the sidewalks that range from small (four by six feet) to larger ones that extend almost an entire city block (over one hundred feet). Surely these were designed and created for a reason, but by whom and for what purpose?

ACKNOWLEDGEMENTS

There are so many people who were involved in this project and integral to making it happen that it is hard to know where to begin. This was more than a master's thesis subsequently leading up to this book; it was a University of Montana multiclass project, a field school, a very public project involving so much of the Missoula community and a labor of love from all. I have jokingly said in the past that my acknowledgements section could easily be just as long as the book itself. There are many people who truly deserve to be recognized.

When I first began my graduate program, I set out to do a very different project—one that I wrestled with around every turn (unsuccessfully) for over a year. When the concept of studying "underground spaces" came along in the fall of 2012, I knew right away (after a brief consideration of "but… *spiders*!") that this was what I needed to do.

So, first and foremost, I would like to thank my entire thesis committee for their never-ending patience with this project: Dr. Greg Campbell, for not throwing me out of his office even once for three years, for his special brand of kindness any time I showed up to his office in exhausted tears and always making time to not only be an academic advisor but also a professional and personal mentor; Dr. Kelly Dixon, for bringing this topic to the 2012 archaeological survey class in the first place, not knowing what Pandora's box was about to be thrown wide open, and then sticking with the project in such a dedicated way that has been above and beyond the call of duty. She often feels bad and jokes about her ruthless edits, but this book would not be in the shape it is in without her, and for that, I am extremely grateful. Thanks to Dr. Pei-Lin Yu, for her dedicated interest in the topic, an endless wealth of pertinent knowledge and for grilling me relentlessly one evening to "form a research question already" until we were shouting at each other and suddenly one finally existed; Mike Monsos, who took my interest in historical preservation and cultivated it into a passion. It became clear as this project rolled along that historical preservation was such an important component, not only as we did the fieldwork but also in regard to the broader picture for future research. I have learned more about historical architecture and practical preservation knowledge and skills from Mike than I even thought I had the aptitude for.

Between the two archaeological survey classes and the summer field school associated with this project, there were forty-two students (within and outside of anthropology) who tackled so much of the research and fieldwork with a fervor that surprised and delighted me on a regular basis. Since it was the very beginning of what would later officially become the Missoula Historic Underground Project (MHUP), instrumental in helping us to understand what we were even looking for were the students of the fall 2012 survey class: Laura Clark, Ashley Deramus, Ryan Dudgeon, Jared Fischer, Mark Gibbons Jr., Jeff McLain, Lisa Menery, Jada Molton, Jason Plain Feather, Megan Richardson, Reina Sherman, Shelby Thomas, Jared Tsosie and Gabe Weiss.

The dedication of the summer 2013 field school students cannot be understated: Liberty Barrows, Katherine Dahlberg, Kat Dwyer, Chad Frady, Dylan Kemp, Kate Kolwicz, Neal Lynch, Bill Seifert, Reina Sherman, Ayme Swartz, Mac Taylor, Julie Tompkins, Dane Torgerson and Josh Uecker. These students dealt with the chaos that embodies an urban archaeology field school and the confusion created by having not only one site but multiple in a busy downtown area. They all took it in stride and rolled with the punches on a daily basis.

The final group of students involved was the fall 2013 survey class (aka the Merc Team), some of whom were crazy enough to return from the field school for another round of MHUP insanity: Liberty Barrows, Kelli Casias, Rachel Fife, Katie Goidich, Kailin Hatlestad, Rachel Ingemi, Dylan Kemp, Andrew McElroy, Kristina Oswald, Britt Schlosshardt, Erin Scoles, Rachel Summers, Justin Urbantis and Kristina Walters. This last group of students spent several weeks of class exploring and surveying every corner of the dark, and often freezing, historic Missoula Mercantile basement to help produce some of the high-quality research in this book.

There were other students and staff, who, with unparalleled organizational and leadership skills, managed to always be where I could not; thank you to Mary Bobbitt and Ayme Swartz, who took time out of their own busy schedules to help with this project, and Bethany Hauer, program coordinator for the Montana Anthropogenic Research Cooperative, who always kept the train moving along anytime it threatened to derail completely. I have the highest respect for them as colleagues and as friends.

While I could talk about the special contributions of every single one of the students who helped with this project, there are two I want to thank specifically for their dedication and all of the extra time spent researching and crawling around in dark, dirty places that most people would not attempt to go: Kelli Casias and Dylan Kemp. When I needed extra help with something they were always the first to volunteer—and still are. Their work during the fall of 2013 in the Missoula Mercantile provided essential information about the history of that building that would have never seen the light of day without them. I am grateful for their insight and never-ending energy, as well as their invaluable friendship. This project would not be what it is right now without them, and this book would not exist.

None of this work could have been accomplished without the support of the downtown Missoula business community allowing us to traipse around in their basements and dealing with endless questions about the history of their buildings: the Missoula Downtown Association; John Coffee (Hammond Arcade); Jenny Montgomery, owner of the Montgomery Distillery; the management and staff at the MacKenzie River Pizza Company; Nicole Garr, Nick Checota and staff at the Top Hat Lounge; Derrick Wcislak and staff at the Riverside Café; Jay and Stephanie LaFlesch; Jim Caras and Sarah at Piece of Mind; Rick Wishcamper from the Wilma Theater; Chris Sampson, superintendent of the Florence Hotel Building; Dudley Dana from the Dana Gallery; and Jed Dennison of ZillaState and Octagon Partners, who basically allowed us to make ourselves at home in the Missoula Mercantile and trusted us implicitly with its care and well-being.

We also had a lot of support from the City of Missoula, which thankfully did not consider us a bunch of "pesky kids" causing a disturbance in the downtown area. The Historic Preservation Office was an endless supply of support and information: Philip Maechling, now retired Missoula historic preservation officer, whom I always teasingly "blame" for starting this whole endeavor, and Leslie Schwab, the current historic preservation officer, who came to this project somewhere in the middle and rolled up her sleeves immediately to help in any way she could. Other groups that have been extremely supportive are the Missoula Historic Preservation Commission, the Missoula Public Library, Nicole Webb and the staff of the Historical Museum at Fort Missoula, Richard Gibson and the Mai Wah Society and Old Butte Historical Adventures in Butte, Montana.

There were a few people who offered their professional expertise to this project and helped answer questions, confirm thoughts and hypotheses and sometimes add even more questions than we started with. I want to thank Steve Adler, of Adler Architects Inc., an architect and historic preservation specialist. I could always count on him to come down to a property at the drop of a hat and offer his insights, teach and mentor not only myself but other students as well. Jeff MacDonald is a historic preservation specialist who made multiple visits to properties to help decipher what in the world we were looking at. Solomon Martin and Scott Loken, both historic masons and contractors, took time out of their packed business schedules to offer insight and support, especially in the Merc, as did Dr. Steve Sheriff from the Geosciences Department at the University of Montana.

From the very beginning, this was a very public project, and the support from the Missoula community has been extraordinary. With this project, we had multiple opportunities to hold public events to share the ongoing research with the public, and they would always come out in record numbers. After two years, this still leaves me in awe of their interest, energy and desire to help in any way. This includes the local Missoula media outlets: Martin Kidston from the *Missoulian* newspaper, Sara Gravlee from ABC/FOX Montana, student journalism students from the University of Montana *Kaimin* newspaper, the *Independent* and KUFM radio.

I would like to thank my family and friends who have had to put up with me through this entire ordeal: my friends Rachel and Janis, who were reluctant to let me move three thousand miles away to the mountains of Montana but knew it was a dream and I had to pursue it and have always been there for me even from far away; Casey, who, when we met seventeen years ago, never would have believed this was the future, but "a lot has changed since then," and he is always around for that much-needed random text, e-mail or phone call; Mark, a boss, a colleague, the brother I never had, mentor and friend, who has dried volumes of tears, listened to countless rants, argued with me at my most stubborn, encouraged me and no matter how many times I wanted to give up on myself would never let me and never once lost faith in me; and Derek, whom I have known for only a few short months but who has provided a lot of much-needed support, encouragement and laughter through the last legs of this book's journey.

I particularly want to thank my mom. A few years ago, when I told her I was thinking about going to graduate school, I'm pretty sure she thought I was crazy. I had a corporate career with a decent salary, and I wanted to go back to school for anthropology. Right! Yet she never once discouraged me from the idea, and she has been with me throughout this journey, the ups and downs, the victories and defeats. She is not only my mom but also my best friend, and I love her dearly.

INTRODUCTION

This project has become an integrated academic, scholarly, applied educational, community-based, historic preservation/local government behemoth.
—Dr. Kelly J. Dixon

Project Background

The overall goal of this project was to integrate archival and archaeological evidence and oral histories relevant to Missoula's historic underground, with the intent of providing a fact-based report on the underground features. As casual conversations with the public about the project occurred and resulted in the confident statement that the "Chinese built the tunnels," it became clear that there was a lot more to the study of the Missoula underground than a survey and documentation of some spaces. There was an anthropological question—multiple questions, in fact—to understand the association people make between the Chinese and the underground and if an archaeological survey could provide evidence to corroborate it. It was also a community history. There have been many interviews conducted over the years about Missoula history, politics, commerce, government, agriculture and many other topics, yet no one had ever specifically addressed the underground.

Therefore, the specific goals of the archaeological survey were archival research, documentation of spaces and conducting more formal oral history interviews with those who might have a personal connection to anything related to the underground. This was expected to produce a comprehensive data set composed of city records, the backgrounds of historical buildings with underground features and information about the Chinese community in Missoula around the turn of the twentieth century. Documentation included maps of the underground spaces in selected buildings that would be completed using Historic American Buildings Survey guidelines, as well as the recordation of architectural and archaeological features.

The Historic American Buildings Survey (HABS) was established in 1933 and since then has functioned as a guideline in a standardized format for recording and documenting historic structures.[2] The HABS program is operated by the National Park Service, the Library of Congress and the American Institute of Architects. Even though none of these HABS drawings thus far has been submitted to the federal database held by the Library of Congress, in consideration of the possibility in the future, the standards were followed as closely as resources and the documentation process would allow.

There has been a plethora of studies across disciplines regarding the Chinese in the United States during the late nineteenth and early twentieth centuries, often specifically related to the 1882 Chinese Exclusion Act and its effects.[3] Many of these studies focus specifically on the Chinese population in the American West. With so many people clamoring for riches mining gold and many fighting for jobs along the railroad, the American West seems to have been the center of the strongest anti-Chinese sentiment in the United States at the time.

Whether it stems from the effects of those sentiments or more contemporary opinions of those in the Chinese community and elsewhere about how early Chinese immigrants are portrayed, there has been a small body of literature that addresses the "Chinese undergrounds" in larger cities such as San Francisco, Seattle and north to Victoria, British Columbia. Many of the works mention the underground only as a side note in the history or larger studies of the Chinese experience in these cities, and most encompass a longer time frame than this project.[4] Missoula was first settled in 1866, and the already small Chinese population had dwindled drastically by 1920; thus the timeframe for this project is 1866–1920. Geographically, the focus has been on the downtown business district or what is now considered the downtown historic district. Even more specifically, it focuses on an approximate four-block area.

Units of Analysis

Units of analysis in research are the primary items being studied and provide the basis for data gathering.[5] In this study, there are four subterranean units of analysis that were observed: steam tunnels, non-steam tunnels, basements and sidewalk voids. These are by no means exhaustive, and further research could result in the discovery of additional units of analysis.

The term *underground* has many connotations, the most common being in reference to anything beneath the surface of the ground (subterranean space). Of course, the term also conjures up images of secret activities and delinquent persons committing acts they prefer to be hidden from authorities and the rest of the community. Most often these are of a religious, social, cultural, political or illegal nature, and sometimes more than one of these factors could be involved. The underground spaces in many cities are assumed to be linked to much more nefarious activity than data generally supports. At the same time, the lore exists for a reason. The primary definition used here will be the simplified definition of any "subterranean space."

Steam tunnels are man-made tunnels that run under the city streets with the intended purpose of providing steam to downtown buildings for heat. For this project, steam tunnels are those that either still include steam pipes, designating their intended purpose, and/or those indicated on the city steam tunnel map.

Although there are rumors of a network of tunnels beneath the city streets, other than steam tunnels, only two other tunnels have been discovered. These are referred to as the *non-steam tunnels*. There is a lengthy tunnel that extends from the

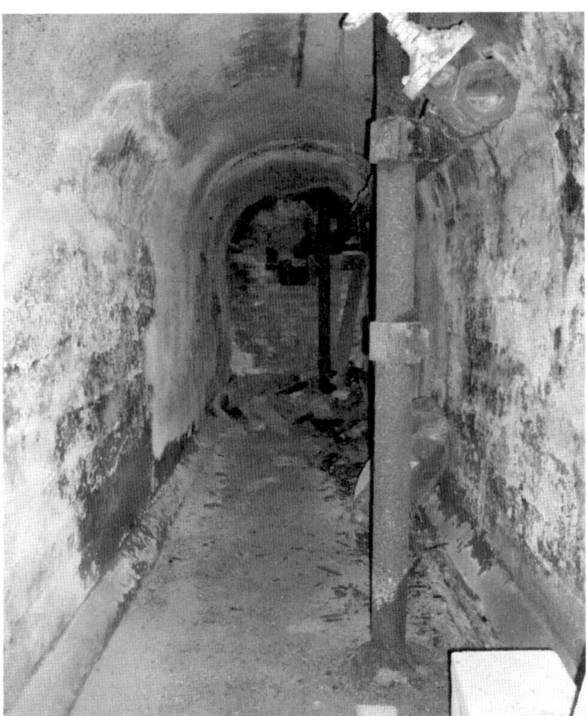

Steam tunnel under Higgins Avenue. *Photo by Jared Fischer.*

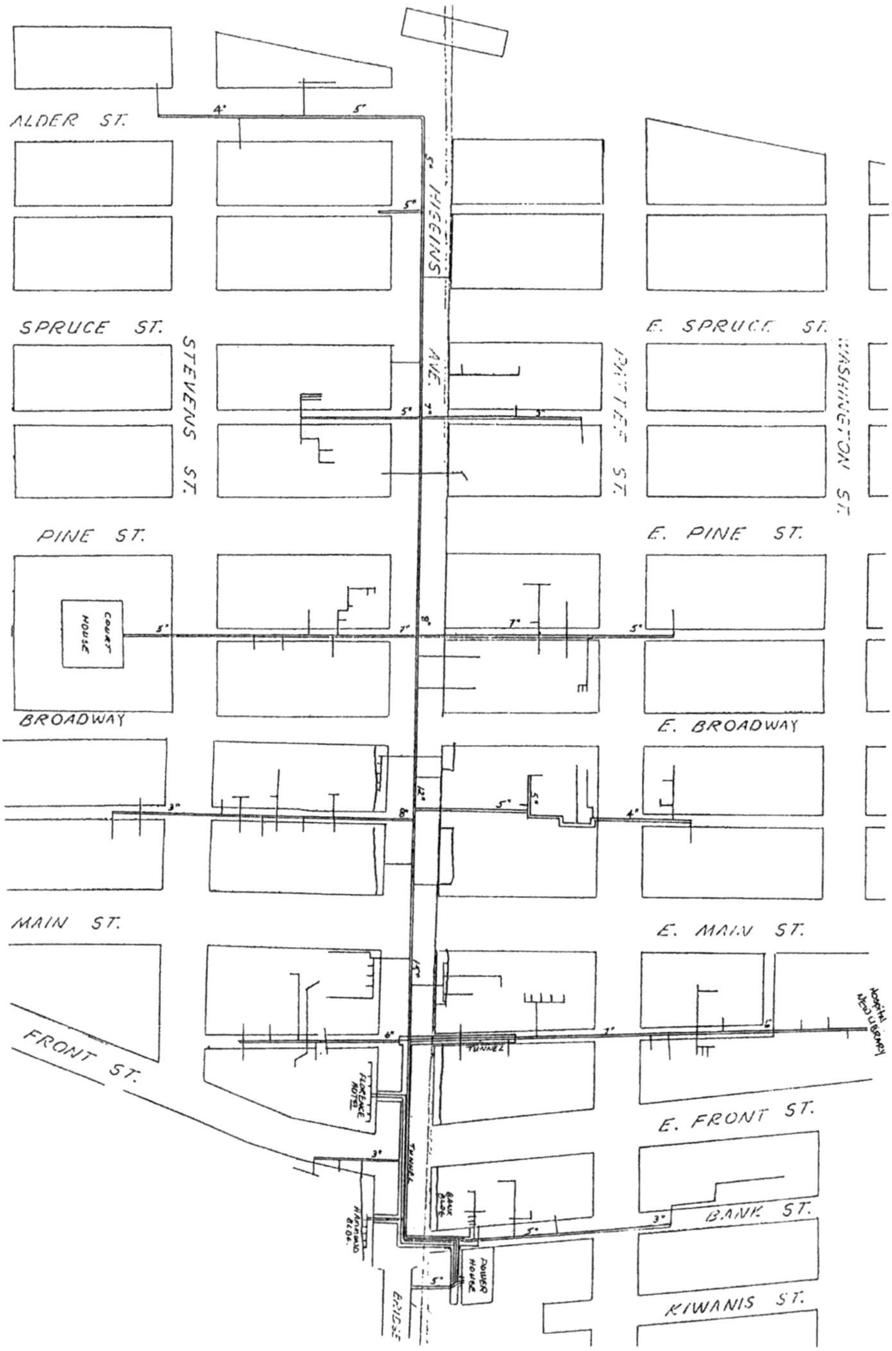

Sketch of Missoula steam tunnel system, date unknown. *Map courtesy of Philip Maechling.*

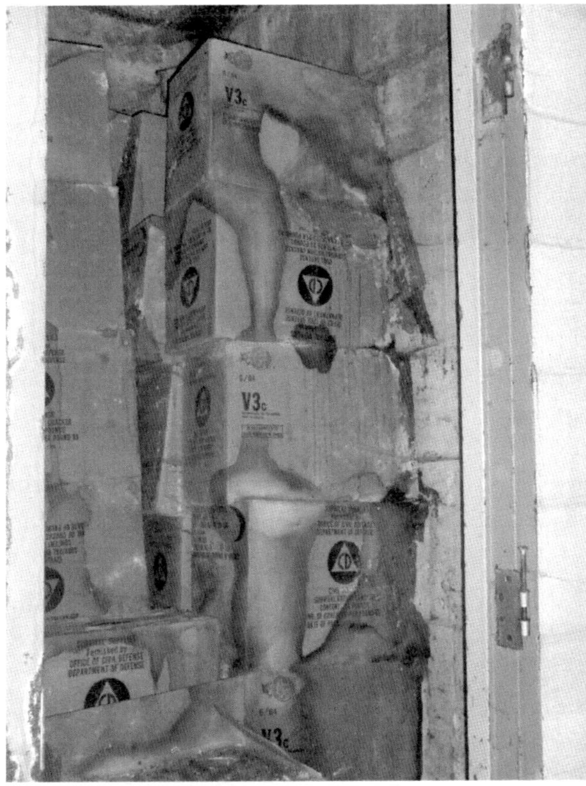

Right: Underground closet full of fallout shelter supplies. *Author's collection.*

Below: Tunnel of unknown use in the basement of the Missoula Mercantile. *Photo by Kelli Casias.*

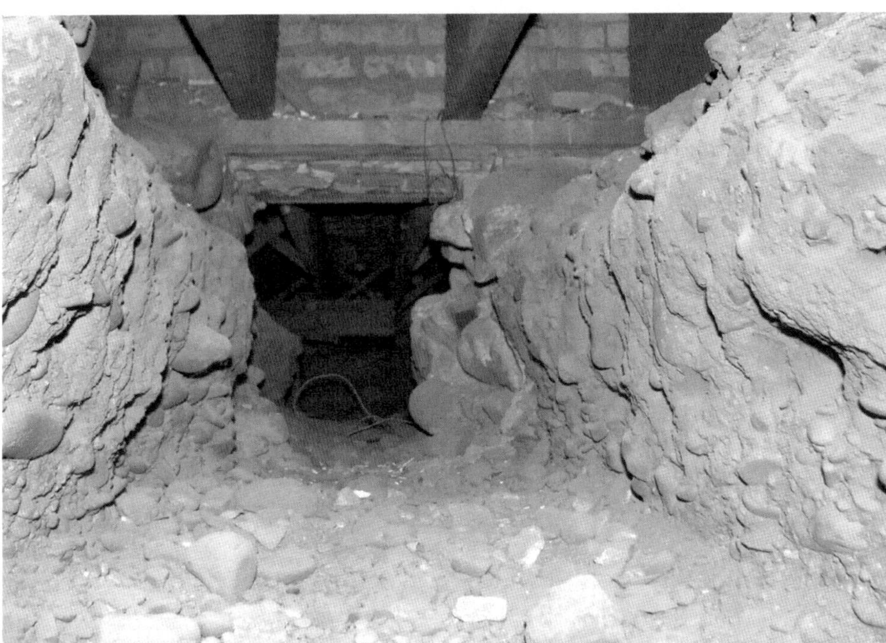

basement of a historic building that was explored but not recorded. While the date of construction and actual usage is unknown, it appears to have been last set up during the 1960s as a fallout shelter. It includes small supply rooms still containing U.S. Department of Defense fallout shelter supplies and water rations from 1964. The walls and ceiling are constructed of massively thick concrete, and there are minimal lighting fixtures. It is very different from steam tunnel construction. More of this type of tunnel may exist in the downtown area. Another non-steam tunnel was discovered and documented in the basement of the historic Missoula Mercantile at 101 South Higgins Avenue during the fall 2013 archaeological survey class.

Basement spaces are any subterranean spaces containing archaeological and architectural features, particularly those that connect to steam tunnels, sidewalk voids and/or where arched or non-arched doorways "to nowhere" have been found. Basement spaces are located under most businesses in the downtown Missoula area. While the basement spaces themselves are not unusual, particularly in an urban business district, the features consistently found within them are of interest, including those with doorways that once led or still lead into rooms under the sidewalks and other unknown locations.

These rooms under the sidewalks represent the fourth unit of analysis, *sidewalk voids*, sometimes referred to as sidewalk vaults. The voids are

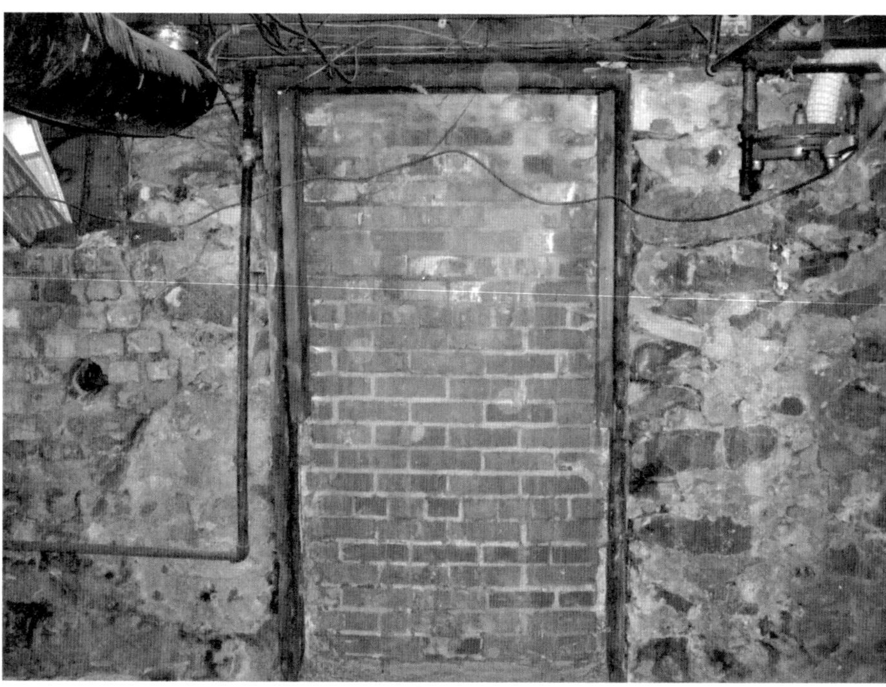

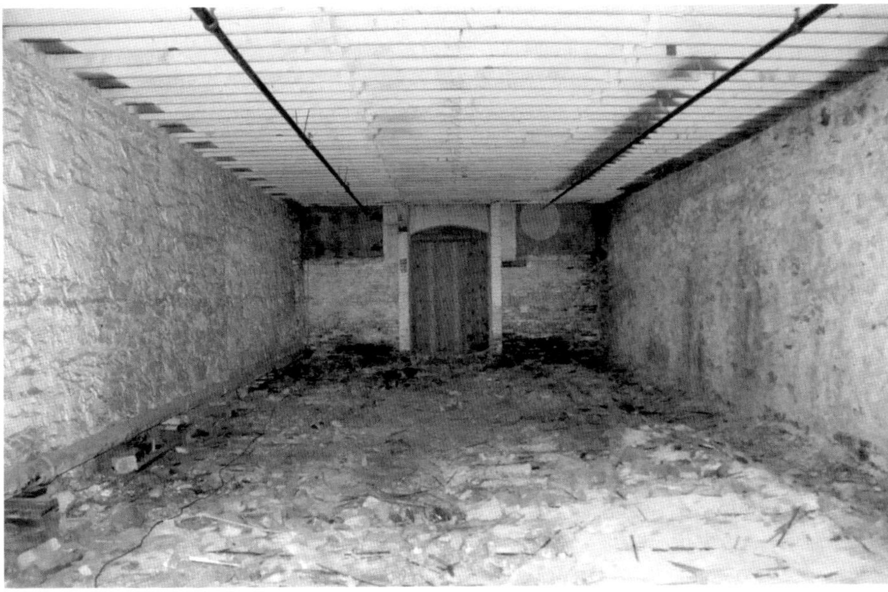

Above: Door and windows in the basement of the Missoula Mercantile (Garden City Drug) that once led to an underground sidewalk void. *Photo by Bethany Hauer.*

Opposite: Bricked-in underground doorway in the basement of Piece of Mind. *Author's collection.*

particularly significant, as they represent some of the more mundane realities (i.e., storage) of underground features that have somehow become rather sensationalized as opium dens and prostitution cribs. There is evidence, however, that some of these sidewalk voids contained small businesses and that some of the larger ones were at one time structurally connected from business to business within a city block. The bulk of sidewalk voids with doorways have been sealed; many of the voids themselves have been filled in for safety and structural reasons.[6]

It is hard to imagine having an actual business in such a dark space underground, let alone people using it as a means of passage, but in most cases they were not feeling around in the dark. It was common for the area to be lighted from the street through glass blocks in the sidewalk above. From the vantage point of walking on the sidewalk, they looked like smooth, square blocks, but underneath they were prisms that would disperse the light over a large area instead of just focusing it downward like a flashlight. Unfortunately, as they crack, break and fall into disrepair, they are often removed, as is the case for all sidewalk lights in Missoula.[7]

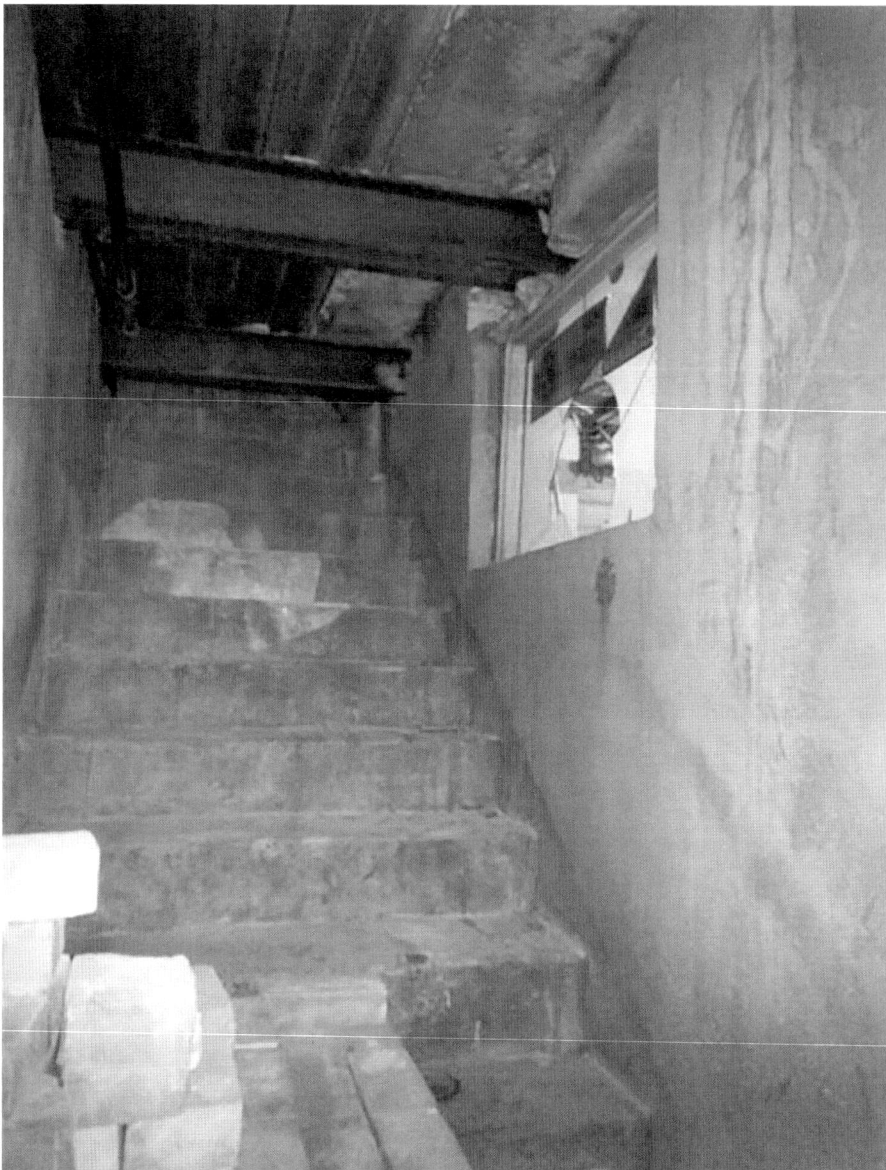

Above: Sealed sidewalk void entrance showing the stairs down from the street and window into the basement business. *Author's collection.*

Opposite, top: Remnants of sidewalk void lights in Butte, Montana. *Author's collection.*

Opposite, bottom: One intact square prism from a section of sidewalk void lights in the Missoula City Surveyor's office after removal. *Photo by Reina Sherman.*

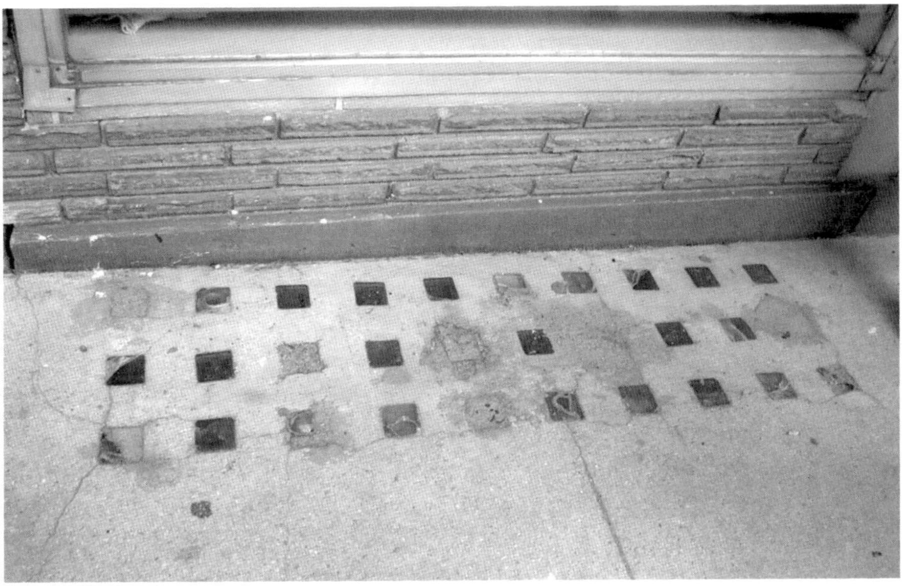

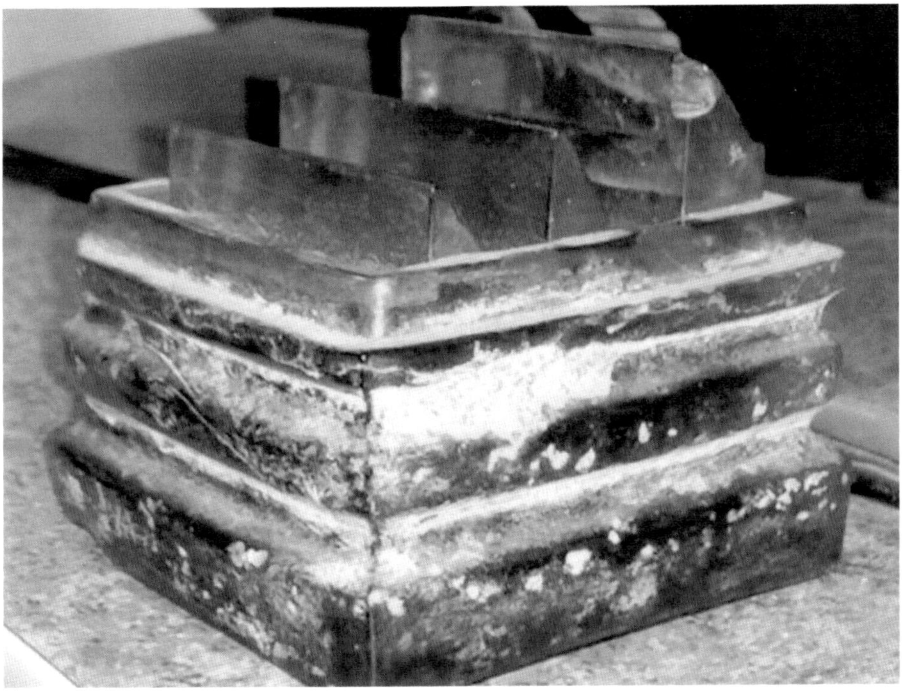

The following chapter will provide a brief glimpse into the urban undergrounds of cities other than Missoula and provide more detail about the methods and data gathering procedures that were used during the Missoula Historic Underground Project. Chapter 2 provides the details of findings for each of the eight properties surveyed: the Hammond Arcade, Top Hat Bar, MacKenzie River Pizza Company, Montgomery Distillery, Riverside Café, Piece of Mind, the LaFlesch Building and the Missoula Mercantile. Chapter 3 discusses the Chinese immigrant experience in the American West and explores the idea of a "Chinese underground." Chapter 4 attempts to weave all of the information from the prior two chapters together to form an understanding thus far of the Missoula historic underground and presents the "authentic Chinatown" concept as a possible origin for underground lore. Chapter 5 looks down the road at possible future research directions in urban archaeology with regard to underground spaces and the overseas Chinese.

1
URBAN UNDERGROUNDS AND THE MISSOULA HISTORIC UNDERGROUND PROJECT

The truth is it's been a long time since I have seen the underground in terms of dirty basements.
—*William Speidel,* Sons of the Profits

In the 1973 book *Longtime Californ'*, Victor Nee and Brett de Bary Nee conducted a multiple-year documentary study in San Francisco's Chinatown in which they say the "old-timers" resented the "exotic" stories about them from the early 1900s. Speaking with Gim Chang, a retired rice merchant, the researchers asked about underground tunnels. "Gim exploded," they said.

> *You read about underground tunnels in old Chinatown? I know nothing about them. I'm quite sure they didn't exist at all. When I was a boy, you know, I used to follow the older boys everywhere and I knew all the dirty, secret places. When white people come to Chinatown looking for curiosities I used to tag along behind the Chinese they took as guides, but I never saw an underground tunnel. Just mahjong rooms in the basements.*[8]

David Lai describes places in the Chinatown of Victoria, British Columbia, where non-Chinese were always expecting to find nefarious activities and told stories about what actually took place—above ground:

> *These interconnecting passageways, closed off from public view, led to tenements, opium dens, gambling clubs, and other socioeconomic activities. Interior courtyards, which served to provide open spaces, light, and ventilation, were entered through gaps between small lanes, or through narrow corridors of tenement buildings. Outsiders could not find their way out once they entered Chinatown; its streetscape or landscape was similar to an ancient Chinese town with a maze of alleys and narrow lanes.*[9]

Underground tours in Portland, Oregon, tell similar tales of opium dens and prostitution, along with the added excitement of stories about "shanghaiing," also known as crimping. According to the tour's website, the tunnels that run along the waterfront and into the downtown area were used for this practice of crimping.[10] Crimping, according to the website, was the practice of kidnapping hardworking Americans who were then sold as slaves to captains of ships "bound for the Orient." In Pendleton, Oregon, there are stone walls that create underground passages around buildings, and the Chinese community is said to have built these passageways as well as retaining walls in some of the residential neighborhoods.[11] Of course, according to guides for the underground tours there, the underground spaces were used as opium dens and for prostitution.

Moving away from opium, gambling dens and shanghaiing for a moment, consider underground cities and tunnels elsewhere in North America that are not generally associated with the Chinese, such as in Seattle, Sacramento, Chicago and the small Moravian town of Nazareth, Pennsylvania. After the Great Seattle Fire of 1889 destroyed thirty-one city blocks, the city streets were regraded one to two stories higher than the original grade, creating a downtown network of underground passageways and basements that had previously been ground level and bustling on the mid-nineteenth-century urban landscape. Of the Seattle underground, historian William Speidel said:

> *I see the big fire that made the underground possible in the first place…not in terms of the flames licking away at the buildings—that kind of thing has been written about ad infinitum, ad nauseum in existing histories—but in terms of the human emotions and the greed and the derring-do which the fire invoked.*[12]

In Sacramento, a rainstorm flooded the entire valley in January 1862. It was the largest storm in recorded history, and many of the city's residents, including the city government officials, fled for San Francisco. Others were

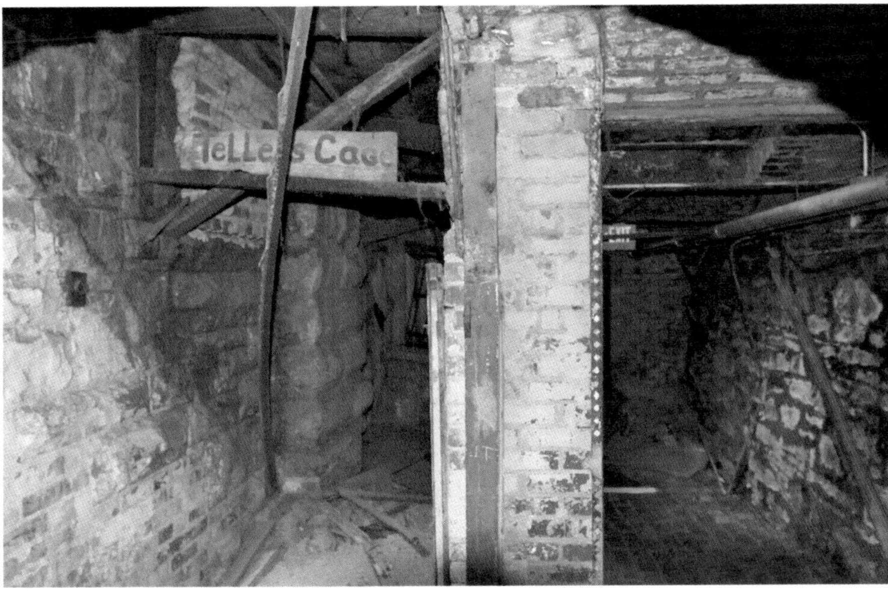

Portion of the Seattle underground that can be seen on the public tour. *Photo by Rennett Stowe, distributed under a CC-BY 2.0 license.*

not so willing to give up and decided to reroute the rivers and raise the buildings above flood level with heavy industrial jackscrews (house jacks). This "fix" created the Sacramento underground. On average, the streets were raised approximately ten feet. These created spaces, now basements, were used for storage, as well as store space.[13] Raising the city's buildings with hydraulic jacks was also part of the solution for poor drainage and bacteria-ridden standing water that caused cholera and other epidemics to run rampant in Chicago.[14]

The town of Nazareth, Pennsylvania, was settled in 1741. Ironically, this small Moravian town in eastern Pennsylvania appears to hold the most similarities to the underground in Missoula. Similar to Missoula, local lore suggests one thing, and historical documentation and survey suggest another. While in Missoula it is suggested that the tunnels were built by the Chinese and underground spaces were used as opium dens, brothels and for Prohibition-era smuggling, in Nazareth it is said that the underground was used for protection from Native Americans, the Underground Railroad and Prohibition.[15] Also similar to Missoula, archival documentation of Nazareth's underground spaces is sparse and relies heavily on local lore.

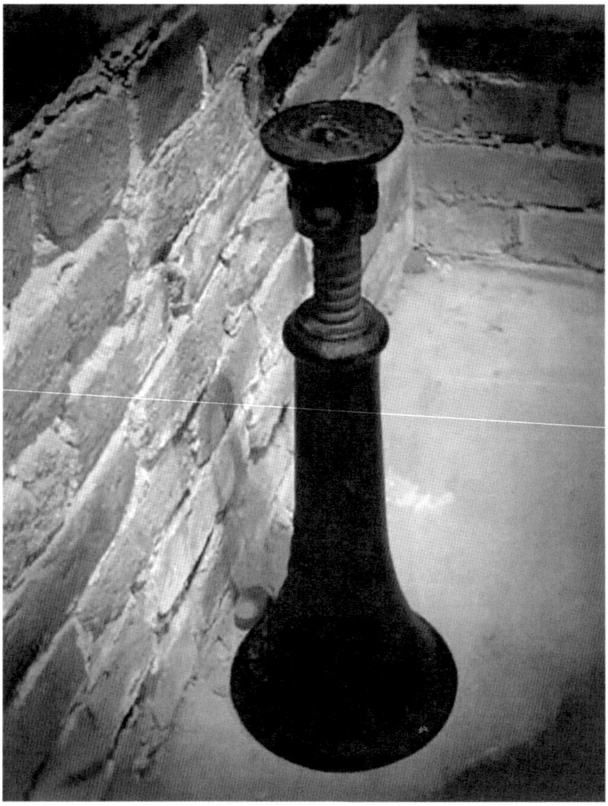

Left: Example of the industrial jackscrews used to raise and level out the buildings in Sacramento. *Photo by Kathryn McAlpin of Historic Old Sacramento.*

Below: Portion of the Sacramento underground that can be seen on the public tour. *Photo by Brandon Darnell of Sacpress.*

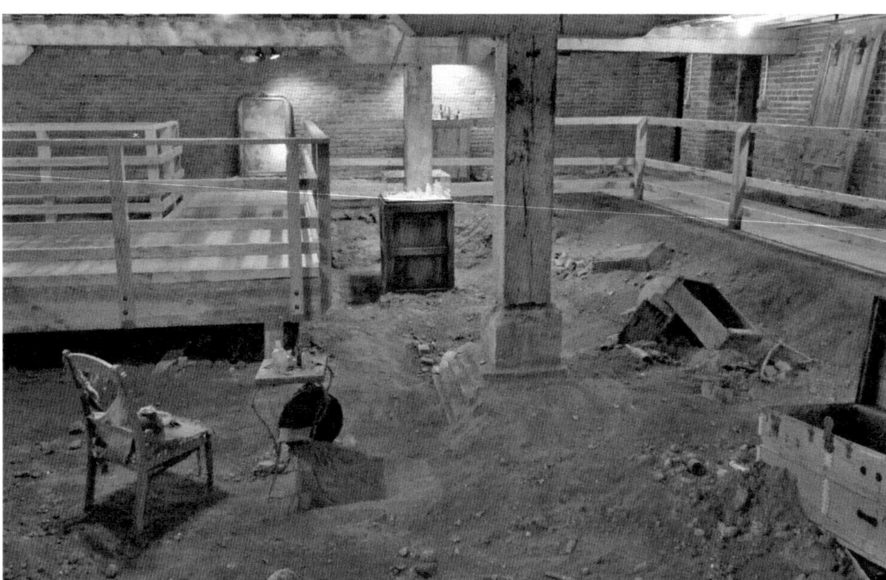

The survey conducted in Nazareth describes tunnels used for public utility—steam, water and so on—as evidenced by photos with intact pipes similar to those in Missoula's steam tunnels. Unfortunately, there are no tunnels to compare with Missoula, only the pipes. The Nazareth study also describes multiple basements with rooms projecting under the sidewalk and blocked doorways that face under streets—sidewalk voids. Turdo suggests that these "room-like projections, which extend from the front of the building under the sidewalk toward Main Street," might have been used as coal bins, due to the presence of coal on the floor, or roll bins for deliveries and notes that some of these rooms connect to one another for ease of servicing.[16] In some cases, the same is true in Missoula, but these explanations do not completely address the extent of sidewalk voids in Missoula or the documented existence of businesses in these sidewalk spaces. Nevertheless, the similarity of Nazareth's and Missoula's underground landscapes is noteworthy, especially when considering these features within the context of urban ecosystem development.

Spatial analysis and landscape studies are useful to understand and document adaptation to dynamic urban ecological environments. In order to do so, it is necessary to define "urban" and how that may be relevant to long-term planning and decision making.[17] Setha Low's anthropological description of the city defines "urban" in terms of everyday "macroprocesses," instead of as a thing or "category."[18] The landscape embodies the past—who, what, when, where, how and even the why.[19] It is both born of experience and creates experience and changes through time and space. Different groups come to the same space, and "influenced by the terrain and by each other, they create new cultural landscapes."[20] Researchers have the ability to combine multidisciplinary approaches—architecture, history, geography, anthropology—to examine how people turn space into place, how they create the landscape and navigate it.

The Missoula Historic Underground Project

Each downtown Missoula property was different from another, so the primary objective for data collection and analysis was to compare data from each of the examined properties. Seeking themes to interpret from the data was preferred because, due to each site's unique features, consistent quantitative data was not possible to collect. This was also such a public and community project, and it was crucial not to force an archaeological hierarchy but instead to foster an environment of collaboration to guide interpretations about general patterns associated with Missoulians' historic (and present) uses of their underground urban landscapes.[21]

Because it was not possible within the scope of this project to survey the entire downtown area, a representative sample of eight sites was used based on location and building history. All of the sites were chosen for their early existence in Missoula and because of their location at the center of town. Three sites were specifically chosen because of their supposed connection with the Chinese immigrant community. One site, the Missoula Mercantile, was chosen because at that time it was the center of Missoula life, business and industry, and much of the city infrastructure originated from there.

The stages of the project were not, in the beginning, set up to work out the way they did. During the initial phase, it was planned that a fourteen-week project in the fall of 2012 would provide a good idea about many of the mysteries of the underground by the time it was complete. After the first full day in the field, it was determined that the whole downtown would be too much and that focusing on the main historic thoroughfare—Front Street—would be the best course of action. After another day in the field, it was realized that the class would need to be divided into three groups, and each group would take a property; one group managed to do two adjacent properties. Thus, our first survey provided data from four Front Street properties' underground spaces by the winter of 2012–13.

At the completion of Phase 1, each group produced a report about its property including a historical overview, methods used, data analysis and recommendations for future work. The groups also observed that the Downtown Missoula National Register of Historic Places (NRHP) nomination paperwork and the site history records on file with the State Historic Preservation Office required updating. The research and fieldwork were able to serve this purpose as well, since project participants were tasked with completing additional historical information for the NRHP files for these properties. For archival research, students primarily made their own choices about what to search for. At this early stage, it was still unclear where it was necessary to focus effort. In subsequent student excursions to the K. Ross Toole Archives in the University of Montana Mansfield Library, specific collections were chosen ahead of time based on previous research. During all archival research, collections were mined for data about building histories and city infrastructure (tunnels, sidewalk voids, construction, business ownership and so on).

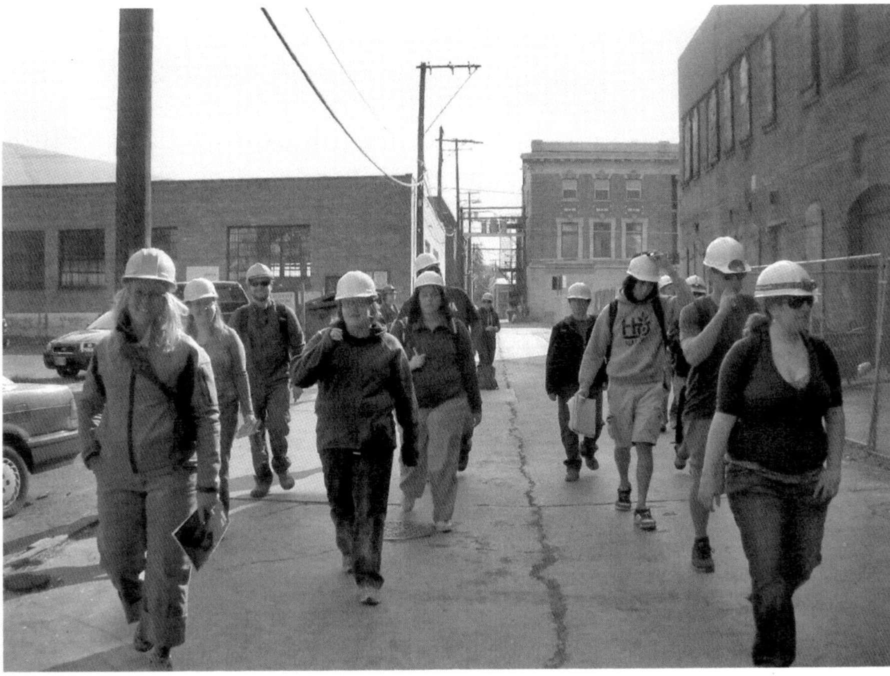

The 2012 archaeology survey methods class from the University of Montana. *Photo by Kelly J. Dixon.*

We also searched for specific notations about the Chinese, social and ethnic group or personal interactions, conflict and informal social control in city documents, personal collections and local newspapers. While this phase was specifically geared toward collecting historical information, there was, however, an effort to be creative in the interpretation of documents—not creative as in making things up, but to use documents that were created for another reason to answer questions for this study. For example, the purpose of the 1981 Basement Encroachment and Sidewalk Obstruction Study was to check the structural integrity and security of the sidewalk voids in the downtown area and make suggestions for improvement.[22]

For our project, this primary document was used for pinpointing where those sidewalk voids are or used to be located, exact dimensions and other pertinent information about their construction. The Sanborn Fire Insurance Maps and the Basement Encroachment and Sidewalk Obstruction Study for the Missoula Central Business District were referred to constantly for understanding a building's footprint, changes, use, whether or not there was a basement or sidewalk void (intact or not) and how it fit into the overall underground infrastructure.

One of the most frustrating limitations with the Sanborn Fire Insurance Maps was being aware of possible inaccuracies and omissions, often based on the cartographer's point of view. This made it difficult to make certain conclusions with absolute confidence. Some structures are labeled simply as "Chinese," while others are labeled with names of businesses (e.g., Florence Hotel) or with a description of their function (e.g., store, hotel, female boarding). The "Chinese" sites were the only structures given an "ethnic" label. Angele Smith examined ordinance survey maps created in Ireland in the nineteenth century, noting how those who made the maps had the power and control of those images.[23] Smith states that "maps do not, indeed cannot, mimic the 'real' world" and that "the map is an excellent artifact of the cultural perception of the surveyor."[24] She goes on to say, "Maps are political tools that attempt to control knowledge…and the knowledge of place and identity."[25] Other issues such as map style changes over time, illegibility and scale variation affecting spatial accuracy are all general issues as discussed by Alicia Valentino in an article regarding usefulness and cautions for using maps in understanding a site's history.[26]

Phase 2 involved a three-week field school during the summer of 2013 that was designed to build on the existing project. The field school ran every day for a three-week period in June 2013. For this phase, student crews were divided into three groups, each examining three properties. Much of the work conducted paralleled what had been done in Phase 1 with a few differences. Each of the students in the field school was expected to generate a plan map of the basement in which he or she was working, and recording of archaeological features took a much more prominent place in the survey process.

The third phase was conducted from September to December 2013, with another archaeological survey class participating in the Missoula Historic Underground Project's ad hoc "learning lab." The same basic procedures of recording, mapping and archival research were followed as in the summer 2013 field school. This only involved one large property, so the work was divided among three groups, each of which documented sections of the building's basement.

Phase 4 was primarily additional research and lab work required after Phase 3 and analysis. This final phase, conducted from January to August 2014, involved data analysis and artifact cataloguing. Artifact cataloguing was carried out in the Dixon Historical Archaeology Lab at the University of Montana. Artifacts from Phase 3 were cleaned, placed into archival-quality bags and tagged with pertinent information for date collected, material type, object description and provenience. Permanent curation has

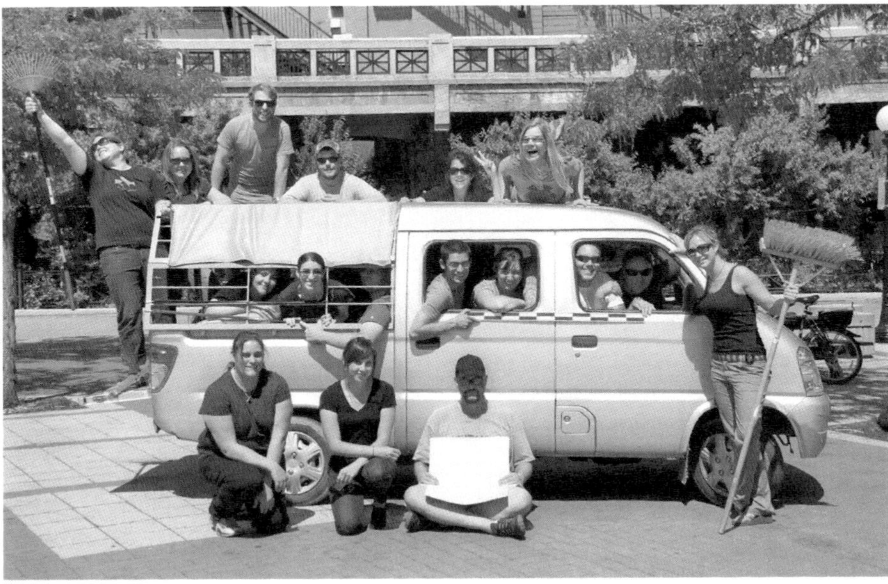

The summer 2013 Urban Archaeology field school crew from the University of Montana. *Photo by Bethany Hauer.*

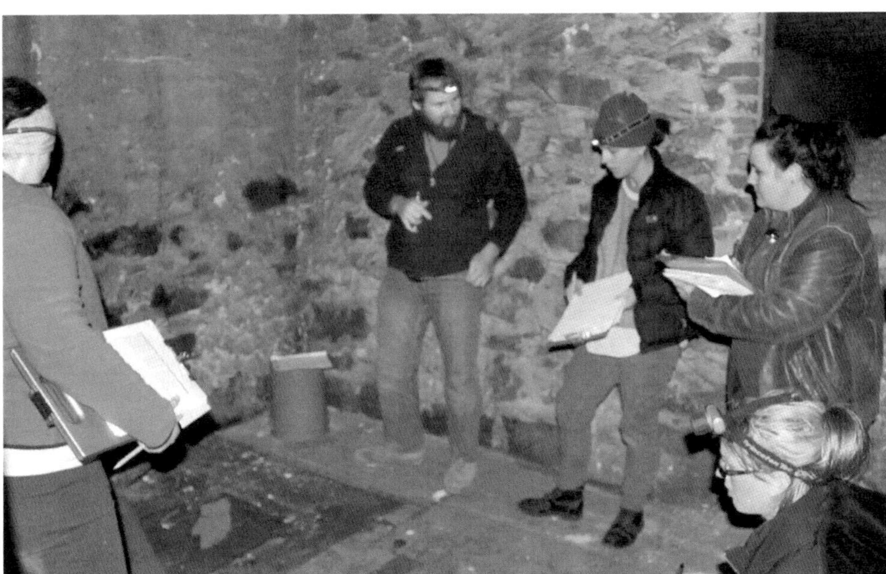

Some members of the 2013 archaeology survey methods class from the University of Montana discussing and recording one of the features in the Missoula Mercantile basement. *Photo by Bethany Hauer.*

yet to be determined. The property from which the artifacts were collected is privately owned, and the owners will decide whether they want to keep the artifacts. If not, they will likely be curated in the University of Montana's Anthropological Curation Facility (UMACF).

There were a number of people involved in this study, and they represent a variety of different groups. For oral history interviews, subjects were generally individuals who have or had a connection to one of the properties being researched or the downtown historic district in general. These could be people who owned, worked at or frequented a business or someone involved in daily operations downtown (e.g., a former store clerk or the retired chief of police). Subjects were not actively recruited for this project by fliers, advertisements or any other means. Rather, the project started with public education events at which requests were made for information about Missoula's underground history. Within a month of the start of the project, the public was invited to be an integral part of the exploration. A local newspaper article about the project invited the local community to share any stories, photos or items they might have in regard to the underground.

A public event was also held downtown at which people were given a chance to explore one of the most historic buildings in Missoula, the Missoula Mercantile. It occurred a few months into the project, and it was possible at that time to share the initial findings. This was the first of multiple public events that were held not only for creating public awareness and obtaining public support but also to encourage education about the underground other than the Chinese lore with which most were familiar. It also served to improve the quality of the archaeology being conducted by involving the public.

The public was considered to be participants from the very beginning. Being in the middle of the downtown, urban Missoula area, the project was highly visible and high profile. It did produce, in very few cases, public relations challenges. Often, "urban archaeologists must confront…puzzlement, annoyance, or resentment."[27] However, the reactions from the public in Missoula were generally welcoming and enthusiastic, with members of the community engaging in the project with great interest. Without the public support of this project, especially the downtown business community, much of the data presented here would not have been discovered. The public outreach component of the project was always meant to be an educational experience for students seeking to learn more about the role of cultural heritage in sustainable urban planning. As part of this training, the students participated in multiple public informational events and manned a public archaeology/project table on the street (during the summer field school) to address questions

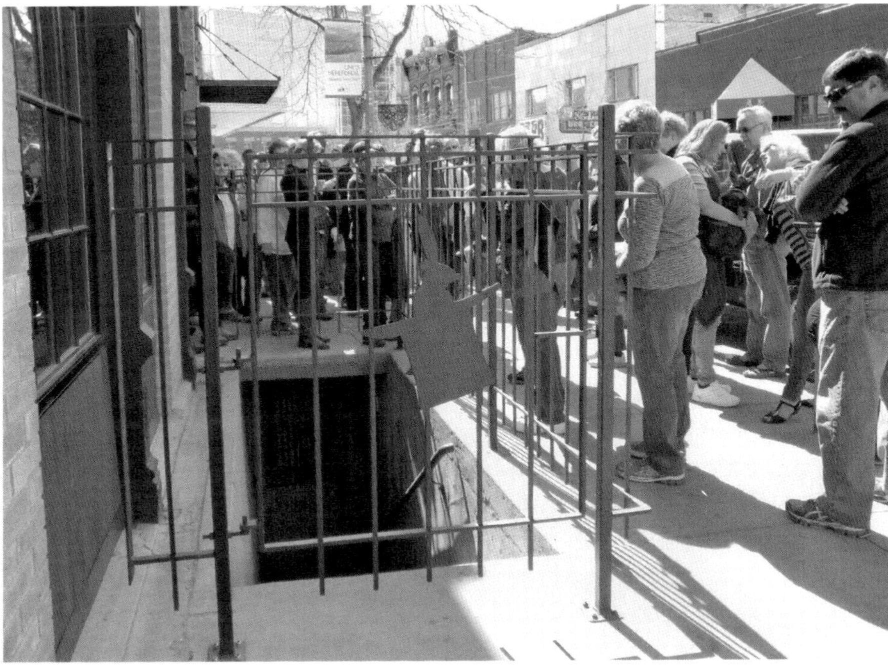

Public tour viewing the sidewalk void entrance to the Top Hat during Historic Preservation Month in May 2013. *Photo by Irene Hesse.*

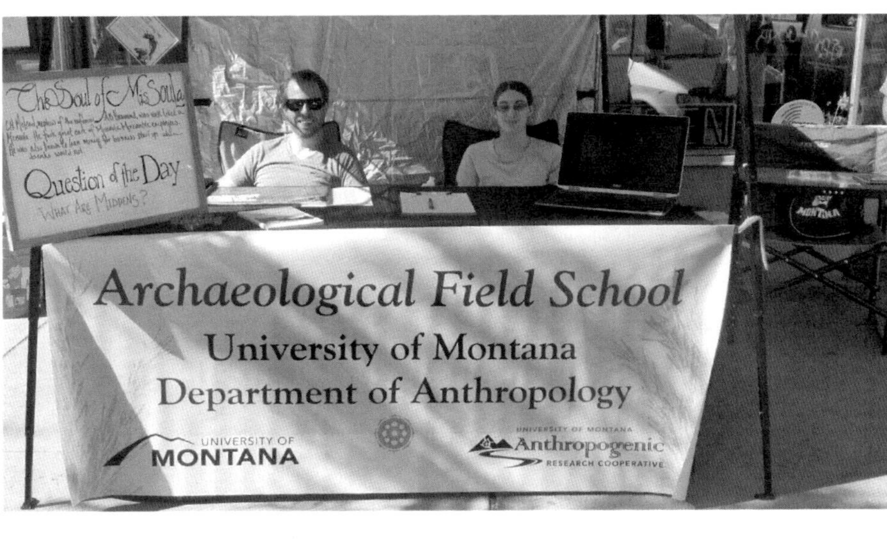

Two students, Mac Taylor (left) and Katherine Dahlberg (right), from the 2013 Urban Archaeology field school participating in public archaeology outreach. *Author's collection.*

about the underground study. They took turns practicing public archaeology by interpreting and presenting project updates to visitors.

Another joy during the course of this project as far as public outreach and education was to have the opportunity to involve the students at Willard Alternative High School in Missoula. Two different classes of social studies students in 2013 and 2014, led by Carolyn Grimaldi and Anneke Hilvert, were able to incorporate the historic underground project into their local history education module. The first group learned about the overall project and the 1870 Missoula urban landscape through project presentations, field trips to the downtown historic district and learning to work with historic documents as primary sources, such as the Sanborn Fire Insurance Maps. The second group also learned about the overall project but focused on preservation, the definition of cultural heritage and how it applied to their lives as part of the Missoula community through related projects at the Missoula Mercantile.

The archaeological survey had two parts: 1) the survey and documentation (mapping) of historic features and 2) the artifact collection. The survey data were analyzed for similarities in design and construction of the buildings

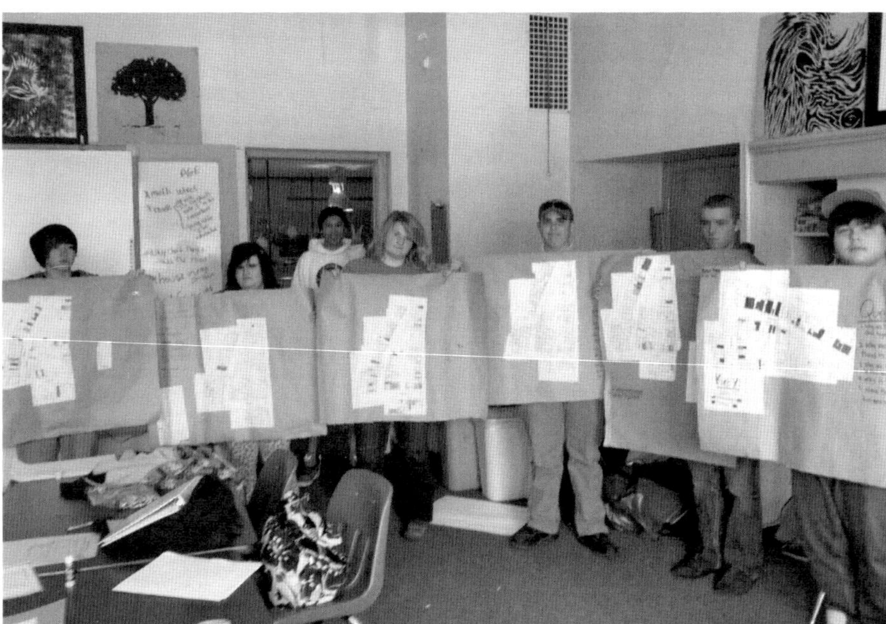

A 2013 Willard High School class showing examples of their Sanborn Fire Insurance Map project. *Author's collection.*

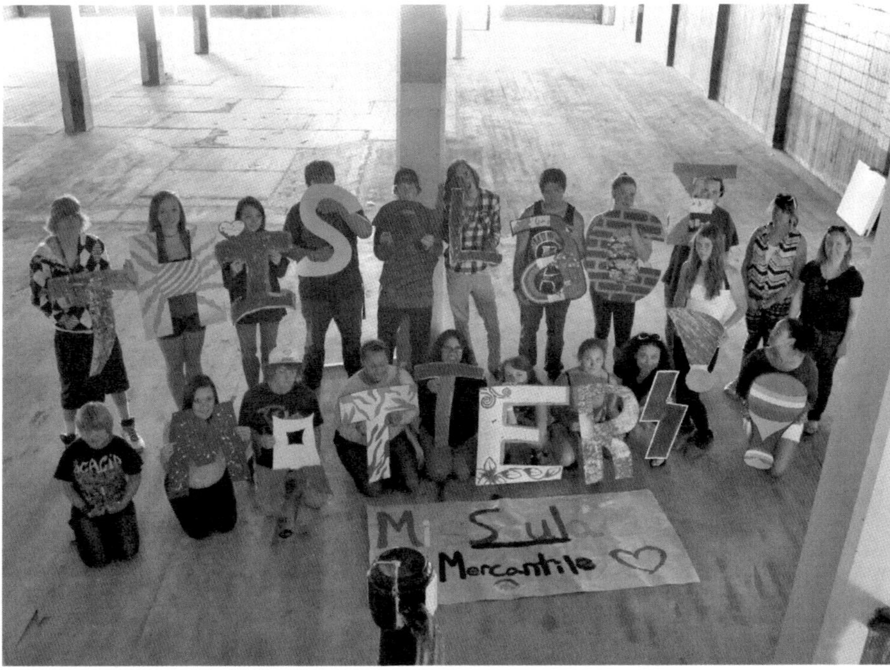

2014 Willard High School students at the Missoula Mercantile with their handmade signs for the National Trust for Historic Preservation's "This Place Matters" campaign. *Author's collection.*

and the "three Fs" of the archaeology of buildings: fabric, form and function.[28] For mapping, measurements were taken and drawings produced according to Historic American Buildings Survey (HABS) guidelines as much as possible. Measurements were taken using an English/metric cloth tape measure despite the HABS guidelines to use metal; the cloth tapes were among our field archaeologists' toolkits and at times much more functional for the spaces in which we were working. Each space mapped was also compared with other city documentation to determine if they connected to or created any underground network. Archaeological and architectural features were recorded at each property. This also included photo documentation, and these features were recorded on the maps. Recorded features were analyzed the same way as the spaces themselves to look for similarities and differences in design and construction.

At one property, MacKenzie River Pizza Company, a small-scale cleanup excavation was performed where the crew screened (with one-eighth-inch mesh) some deposits and debris from the blocked entrance to

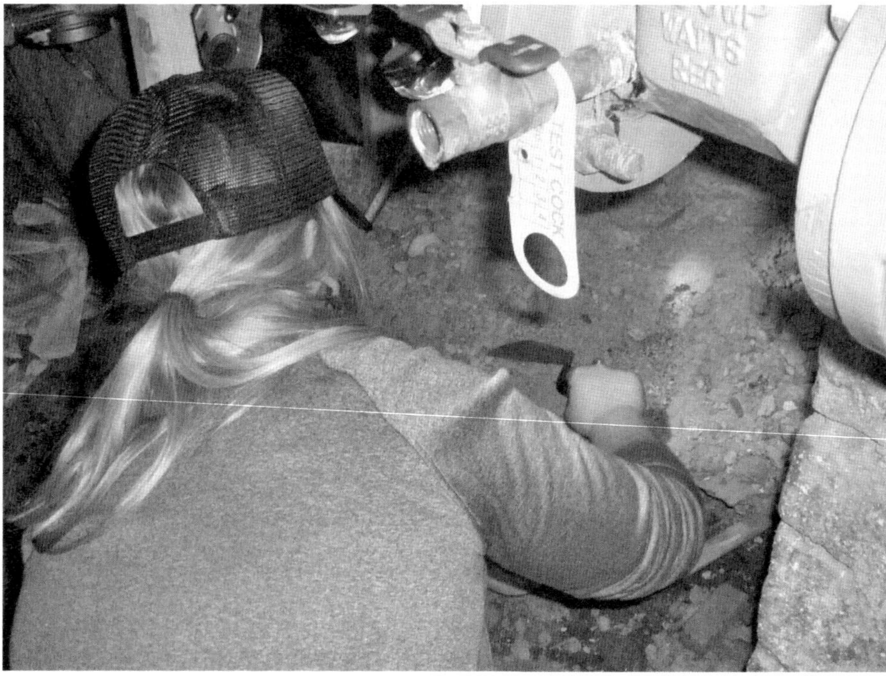

Mini cleanup excavation in the basement closet of MacKenzie River Pizza Company, 137 West Front Street. *Photo by Mary Bobbitt.*

a sidewalk void. At another site, the Missoula Mercantile/Garden City Drug, a surface collection was conducted. In this case, the room was first measured and divided into ten three- by three-meter units. Artifacts were measured and mapped on the surface inventory to document provenience and then collected into brown paper bags. Bags were labeled with site number, date, unit number and the names of those collecting. Artifacts were processed following established lab techniques and protocols for cleaning and identifying the material.

The artifact collection and analysis were not major components of this study for two reasons. First, the artifacts recovered from the small-scale cleanup excavation at MacKenzie River Pizza Company were determined to be quite modern, likely part of the debris used for fill of the sidewalk void after the 1981 sidewalk and void study.[29] Second, the artifacts collected at the Missoula Mercantile and Garden City Drug were not necessarily expected to produce any information to answer the specific research questions of this study due to the nature of objects found and the use of that space as the liquor and tobacco department of the Mercantile. They were, however,

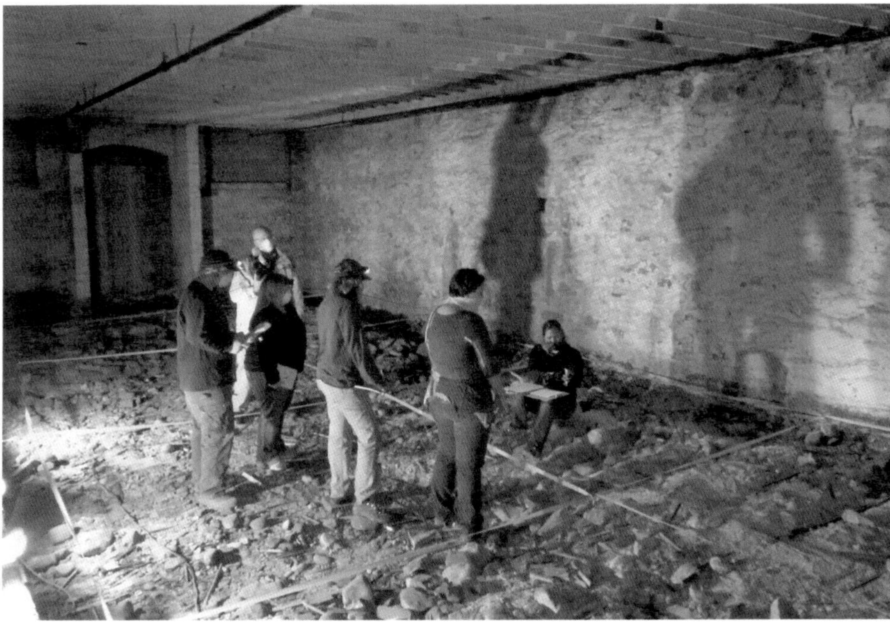

Beginning the artifact surface collection in what was once the Liquor and Cigar Department in the Missoula Mercantile basement, as well as the basement of Garden City Drug. *Author's Collection.*

treated as a possible source of data and not counted out completely. As a study of historical landscape the project was designed to include as many methodological approaches as possible, including artifact collection where prudent.[30] The artifact collection was also carried out as part of an educational experience for the archaeological survey classes.

2
WHAT LIES BENEATH MISSOULA

If you take myth and folklore, and these things that speak in symbols, they can be interpreted in so many ways that although the actual image is clear enough, the interpretation is infinitely blurred, a sort of enormous rainbow of every possible color you could imagine.
—Diana Wynne Jones

This chapter presents the results and analysis of the research conducted from September 2012 through August 2014. Since the eight properties were surveyed in stages, the results are presented in that format, with each property being discussed separately. Each section will explore the historical background and oral history for each property, along with the results of the archaeological survey, including maps and feature documentation. Various forms of historical documentation, archival materials, newspapers, maps and oral histories have been used to pinpoint potential locations of specific Chinese use of Missoula's underground spaces. Additionally, in the interest of attaining multiple lines of evidence, archaeology can give insight into the relatively under-documented lives of Chinese and Chinese American citizens in the American West.[31]

Historical documentation alone makes this research challenging. For instance, as is true in many new urban landscapes, the city grows and is developed and addresses change. This makes tracking of city records, deeds and property ownership, as well as business or residential locations, difficult to follow. Maps change, too. What does not change, unless a structure is massively altered or completely destroyed, is the physical location. Addresses change and businesses and people come and go, but the physical underground associated with a place does not.

For each site, specific attention was given to the construction and property history, business type, features (architectural and archaeological), sidewalk voids and tunnel access possibilities. These are compared and discussed here in terms of the oral history and local lore. Also when possible, the data will be compared and contrasted with some of the literature regarding similar known cases.

Always keep in mind that we wanted to know if it were possible to find an archaeological signature recognizable as distinctly Chinese in the underground spaces. Before embarking on the analysis of all sites, it is important to understand what is meant, in terms of this study, as an archaeological signature of a "Chinese" underground. There have been many opinions and debates in anthropology about identity, ethnicity, race and the ability or lack thereof for finding these in the archaeological record.[32] According to leading historical archaeologist Charles Orser, "easy interpretations rest too strongly on ethnic stereotypes."[33] The aim of this project was to not let this happen in the search for an archaeological signature that endorses much of the lore in Missoula.

Hammond Arcade

The Hammond Arcade has an Art Deco architectural style and is a concrete and brick structure with two floors, one above ground on the north side of the building and one below grade on the south side. This gives the south side of the building the appearance of being ground level because it is directly accessible from the parking area adjacent to the south elevation of the structure. As one moves north into the building, it becomes underground space as the building cuts into the slope toward West Front Street.

Historical Background

The current building that sits on this lot was constructed in 1934 after the original Hammond Building, constructed between 1888 and 1890, was destroyed by fire. The original was a brick and granite castle-like four-story structure. The primary tenant in the building for many years was the Missoula Drug Company, owned by Sid J. Coffee. Missoula Drug occupied

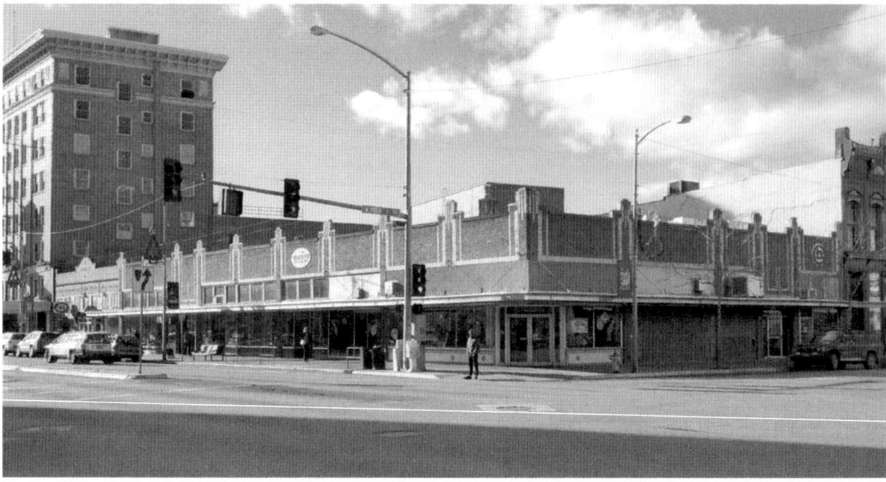

The Hammond Arcade, located at 101 South Higgins Avenue. *Photo by Mark Gibbons Jr.*

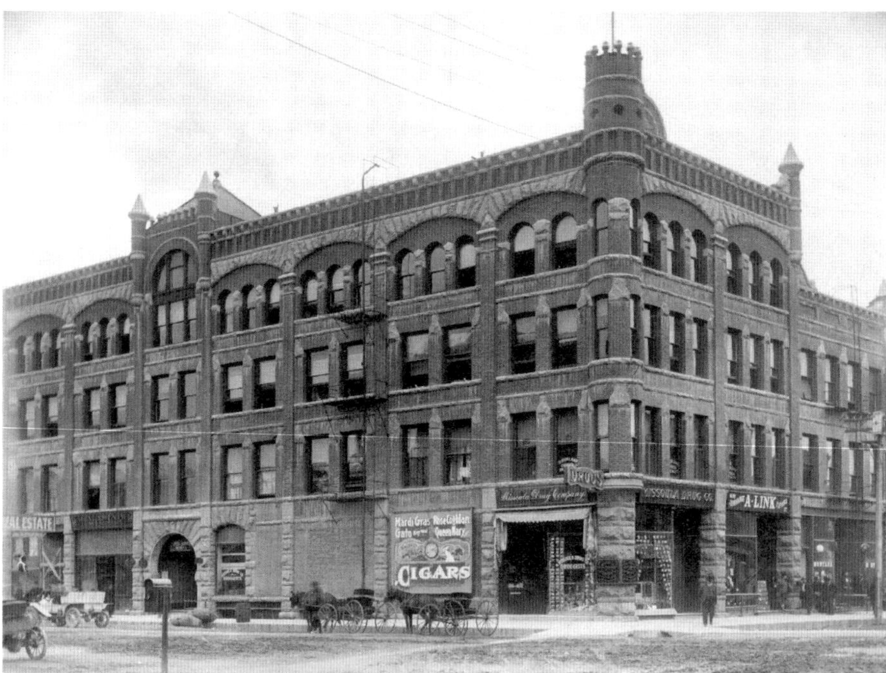

The Hammond Block, circa 1900. *Photo No. 486.047.0083, Archives and Special Collections, Mansfield Library, University of Montana.*

the largest space in the northeast corner of the building and was one of the few sources of competition for the massively successful Missoula Mercantile across the street to the northeast.

From the very beginning and into the present, the Hammond Building/ Arcade has always been a mixed-use building. The earliest Polk City Directory for Missoula that was available lists a painter, saloons, a tailor and furnished rooms in addition to the drugstore.[34] Except for the Missoula Drug Company, which occupied the same prominent space for over seventy years, businesses and tenants of the furnished rooms would come and go. Since this book covers the time period from approximately 1870 to 1920, the main focus is on the original Hammond Building. Starting in 1905, it says that J.W. Kennedy, a plumber, was located in the basement. In 1913, the name changes to H.A. Burke, also a plumber, and then changes back to J.W. Kennedy in 1926. No other business is mentioned as operating out of the basement of the Hammond Building.

The Hammond Building first appears on the 1890 Sanborn Fire Insurance Map as a building still under construction yet already housing five saloons. The building had four floors, a basement and a subbasement except for the lot on the west end, which appeared to be a separate structure yet still part of the Hammond Building complex. This part was three floors with a basement and a subbasement. In the rear of the three-story building were beer cellars for the Missoula Brewery situated to the south of the Hammond. The following year the building was clearly named and delineated on the 1891 Sanborn. Much of the first floor was vacant except for a millinery shop and one saloon. The second, third and fourth floors were used as office space.

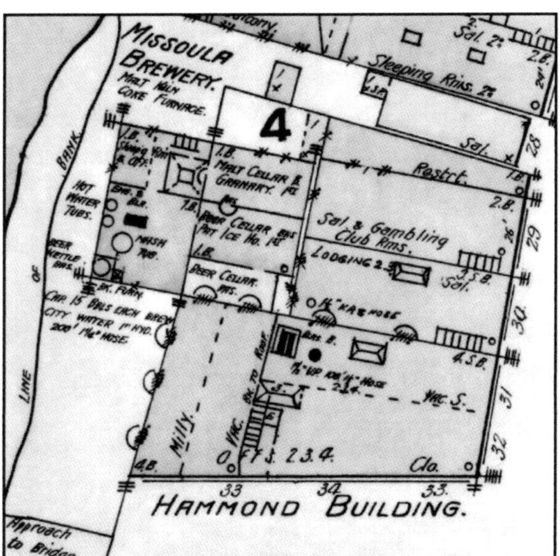

A detail of an 1891 Sanborn Fire Insurance Map in which the Hammond Building appears for the first time. *Map used with permission from Environmental Data Resources Inc.*

By 1902, the saloon was gone; there were offices on the second floor, leaving the

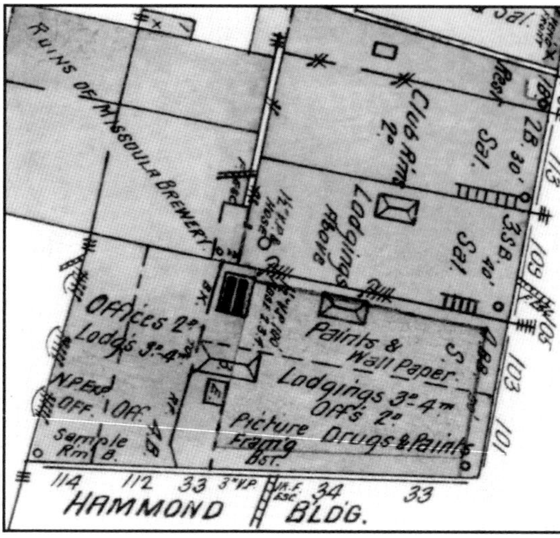

A detail of a 1902 Sanborn Fire Insurance Map of the Hammond Building. *Map used with permission from Environmental Data Resources Inc.*

third and fourth as lodging. Missoula Drug Company was now the primary tenant in the northeast corner. The Sanborn map indicates that the Missoula Brewery was gone by then, labeling the area as "Ruins of Brewery." The "annex" was added by the 1912 Sanborn, taking three more lots to the south facing Higgins Avenue. The plumbing store is shown in the basement.

Archaeological Survey

The Sullivan sidewalk report for the Hammond Building is full of information about the sidewalk void that borders the building on the north (Front Street) and the east (Higgins Avenue). The Front Street length is 71 feet, 10 inches, and the Higgins Avenue length is 128 feet. In 1981, when the report was completed, all of the void space was still open even though all of the street access had been concreted closed and stair access removed. Sections of the void have been completely in-filled now, and the 1981 sidewalk report shows nine separate openings, seven of which are now sealed with concrete.

There are six walls to partition the sidewalk void into separate units. The unit adjacent to the Missoula Drug Company contains a brick arched doorway in the middle. Interestingly, these walls in the voids line up with divisions and support walls of the building above ground. Even though these are under the sidewalk, they appear to be structural extensions of the building.[35] Considering the foundation of the original building appears to have been reused in the 1934 construction, they are likely remnants of the 1888–90 building.

The Hammond Building had an entrance for steam tunnel access, but it was recently sealed and is no longer accessible. This steam tunnel access is located in the Higgins Avenue facing wall of one of the still-intact voids.

Being basically situated across the street from the steam plant, this tunnel is one of the larger steam conduits that allows for a channel that supported the high pressure created by the plant to convey water and steam. Although it was not able to be recorded as a feature, it measures approximately six feet in height and four feet wide. There are still steam pipes in the tunnel that once ran east–west into the building from the main steam tunnel under Higgins Avenue, which runs north–south. There was another branch from the main steam tunnel under West Front Street with three pipes connecting to the Hammond Building—one into each section of the building.

There were a few challenges to mapping the Hammond Building's massive basement space. For example, much of the space is still used as storage for a large and busy restaurant. Other parts of this basement included locked storage for other tenants. For these reasons, it was not possible at the time to make a plan map of the entire space. An extremely helpful document was provided by the current caretaker, John Coffee, a grandson of Sid Coffee. This document was an engineering and architectural plan of the basement

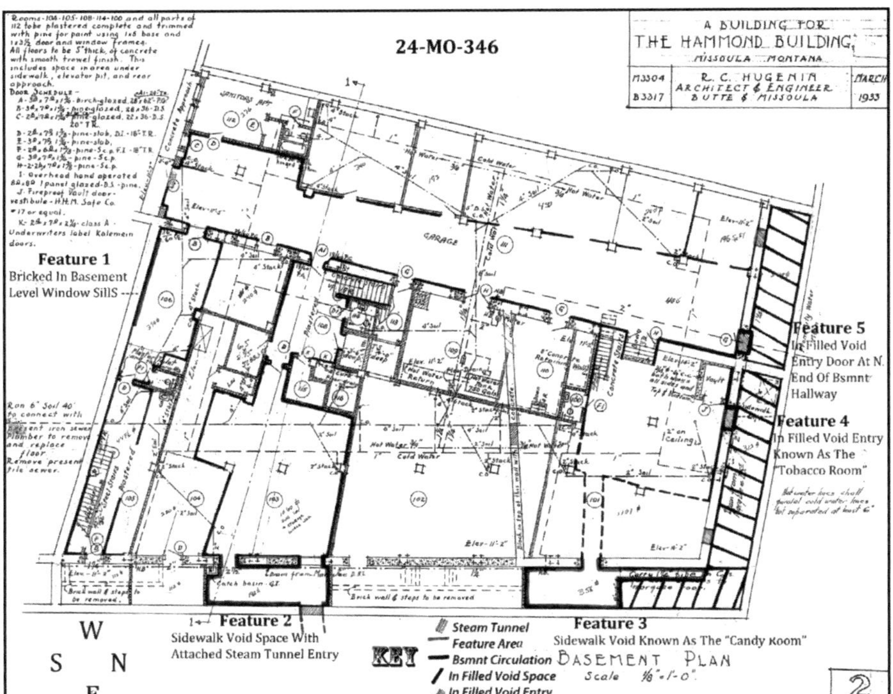

Feature map of the Hammond Arcade basement, using existing engineering plans from 1934. *Engineering plans courtesy of John Coffee. Features mapped by Mark Gibbons Jr.*

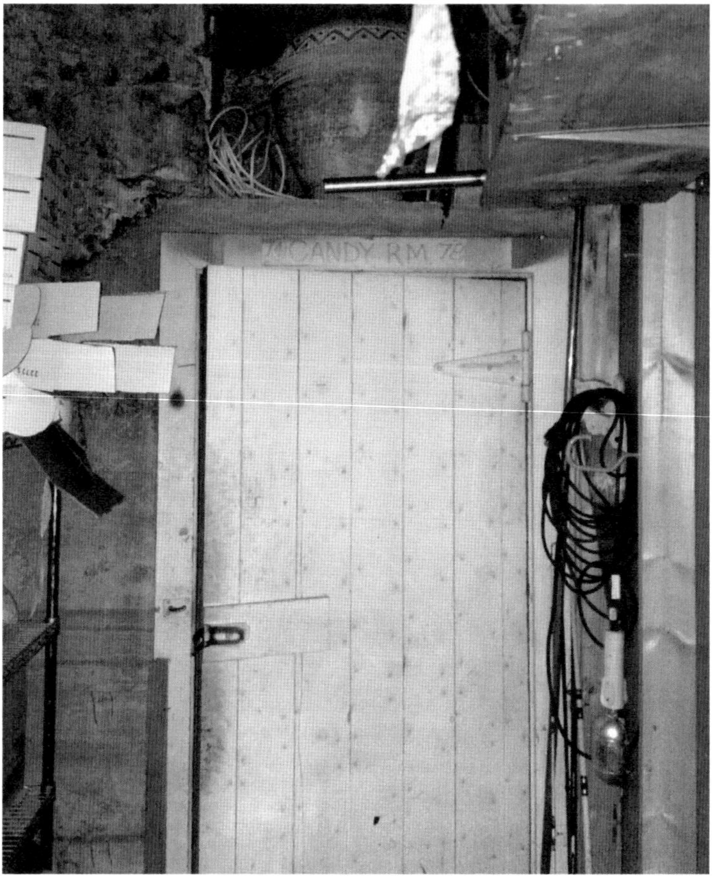

Opposite, top: Hammond Arcade Feature 4 is a wooden double door that once led to the sidewalk void "Cigarette Room" where tax stamps were applied before sale. *Author's collection.*

Left: Hammond Arcade Feature 3 is a door leading to the sidewalk void, which was once used as the Missoula Drug Company's "Candy Room." *Photo by Mark Gibbons Jr.*

from 1933 and was part of the reconstruction plans after the fire. Even though the building was completely destroyed in the fire, the foundation and basement remained virtually intact. The architectural drawing was used as a base for mapping the important features.

Feature 1 consisted of five bricked-in windows in the south wall of the original building, which now is a shared wall for the building next door. Prior to the addition of the neighboring building and redirection of the Clark Fork River, the river once ran just behind the south wall of the building. These windows would have overlooked the river. Features 2 and 3 are both east facing (Higgins Avenue). Feature 2 shows the sidewalk void that provides access to the steam tunnel. Feature 3 was once the "Candy Room" for the Missoula Drug Company. The current business that occupies the building uses the void as storage space. The original door still exists, and a label with "Candy Room" adheres to the doorframe above the entrance.

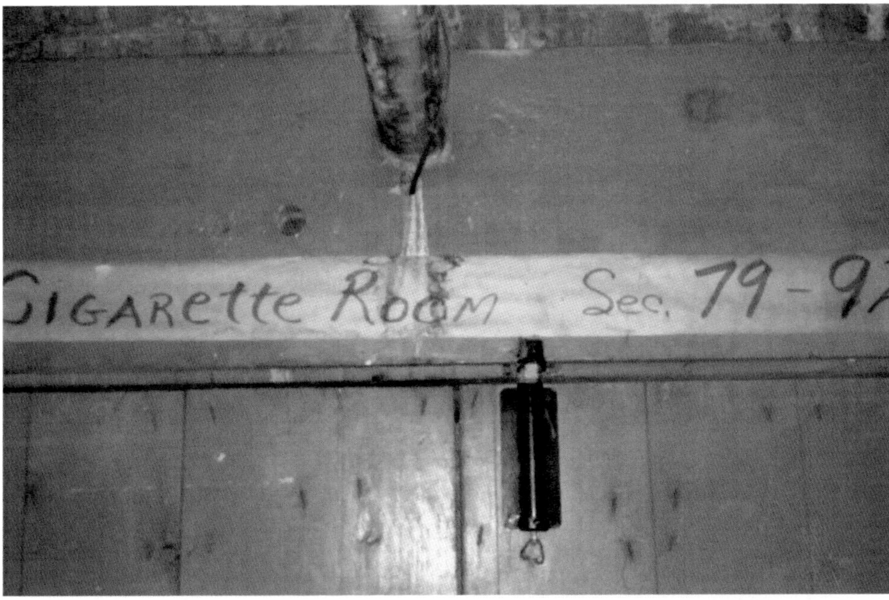

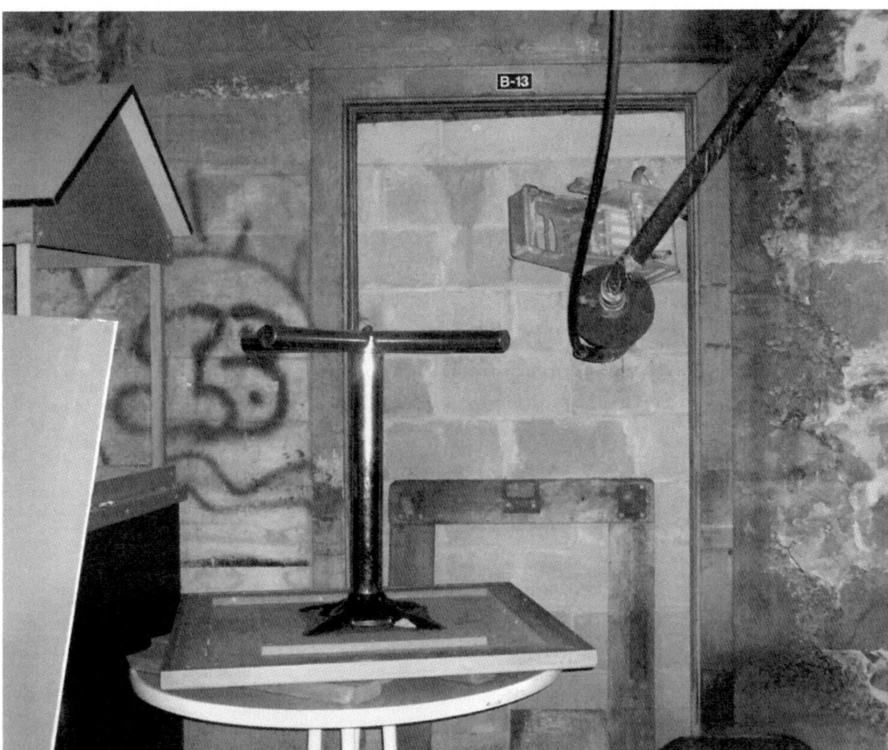

Above: Hammond Arcade Feature 5 is now a sealed doorway that led to the West Front Street sidewalk void, which has also been in-filled. *Author's collection.*

Feature 4 is a double door that once led to a sidewalk void on the north side of the building (Front Street) that is now in-filled. The void was used as a place for stamping the tax on tobacco products and storing grain alcohol. There was also once an elevator lift in this void to the street above for delivery of goods.[36] The label "Cigarette Room" adheres to the doorframe above. Feature 5 also faces north and is located to the west of Feature 4. It is a concrete sealed doorway to another area of the Front Street sidewalk void.

Of all the properties studied for this project, the underground spaces in the Hammond Arcade building appear to have been created and used mostly for public utility, storage and business preparations for the Missoula Drug Company. Although, that cannot be stated with 100 percent certainty since it is no longer possible to see the voids that were filled. The sections of the sidewalk void that remain open are still used for these same purposes today.

Summary Analysis

The Hammond Building/Arcade was designed (1888–90) from the beginning to be a mixed-use building. Following the fire that destroyed the four-story structure, the new construction (1934), a bit smaller, has served the same purpose. In terms of underground space, our fieldwork concluded that the basement, sidewalk voids and tunnel access points appear to have been created and used for public utility, storage and business operations, primarily for the largest and longest tenant, the Missoula Drug Company. The sidewalk voids provided not only access for deliveries to the building but also steam tunnel access in at least two places. The Hammond Building/Arcade utilized three types of underground features (i.e., "units of analysis"), none of which appears to have any connection with the Chinese community in nineteenth-century Missoula.

THE TOP HAT

The Top Hat is a bar and restaurant, known for its live music shows, movie nights and "Family Friendly Fun Night" with programming geared toward the kids. The Top Hat has recently undergone major renovations to add the kitchen in the basement and rear section of the building. Much of the interior changed extensively during the renovation. Our research was conducted just before and at the very beginning of these renovations, making it possible

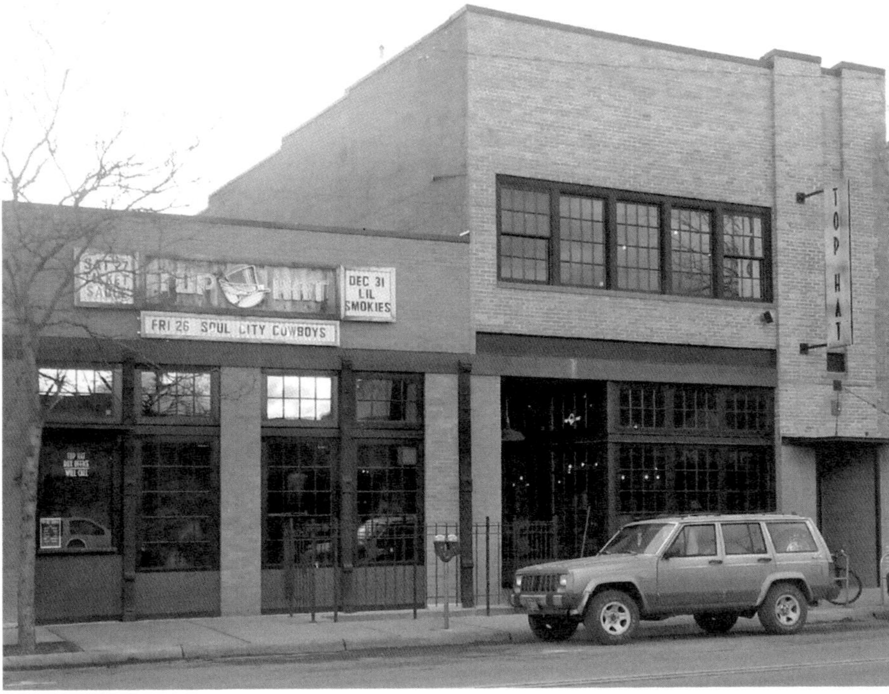

The Top Hat Bar, located at 130 West Front Street. *Author's collection.*

to compile significant historical information from this property before the changes forever altered the historic fabric of the building's basement.

Historical Background

According to the earliest Polk Directory data, this property was a saloon or bar from 1903 to 1917. There are a few years missing of the Polk Directory for Missoula, but in 1925, during the Prohibition era, the building housed an auto supply shop. The earliest Sanborn maps for Missoula corroborate the Polk Directory information and confirm that by 1921 the space was indeed an auto shop. In the years following, the building also housed the Davenport Rooms and the KGVO radio broadcasting station where radio personality Paul Harvey reportedly made his first radio broadcast.[37] In 1956, the Top Hat moved in, and although ownership has changed hands over the years, this drinking establishment has remained in business for over half a century.

The 1891 Sanborn indicates the building was a one-story structure, and the 1893 Sanborn indicates it grew to two stories. In 1893, there were also additions on the east and west sides of the building, incorporating what were two separate businesses in 1891, with an interior wall splitting the building in two. The second floor was not yet complete. It is believed that the original 1879 stone rubble masonry foundation/basement of the building's central core remained intact until the 2013 renovations.

Archaeological Survey

At the time that mapping began in this basement space, the Top Hat had just experienced a transfer of ownership. Until November 2012 the basement area was divided into separate sections. It was primarily used for storage, but at the north end of the basement (closest to the stair access from the bar upstairs), there was a "green room" area for bands playing at the venue. There was a full wall of wooden cabinets in another room adjacent to the band green room and a triple-basin stainless steel sink. Moving south across the basement, along the west wall was a finished bathroom with a cold storage locker covered with plywood on the inside. The southern portion of the basement was used for storage, and the west wall in this area was a stone rubble masonry wall behind corkboard and a long workbench. These were all elements that had been added to the basement in approximately the past twenty-five years.

Looking south, however, there was a rubble archway original to the foundation of the building. Through this archway was the sidewalk void for the property, representing the southernmost part of the building's basement floor plan. Inside the void, a door accessed a set of stairs leading up to the street. There was another small room in the void containing mechanical equipment. This sidewalk void entrance from the street was more unusual than the others; although the sidewalk void existed in 1981 when the Sullivan sidewalk report was conducted, there is no stairway entrance shown on the drawing or referenced in the report.[38] The report does say there used to be a stairway that was removed. Apparently, sometime after 1981, the sidewalk void entrance was restored.

The feature documentation was confined to those features that were known to be original to the building, with the exception of one. During the first visit to the property, Nicole Garr, the daughter of the previous owner, revealed a small metal encasement (i.e., small trapdoor) in the concrete floor. She said that her dad told her that there was a floor latch in this encasement

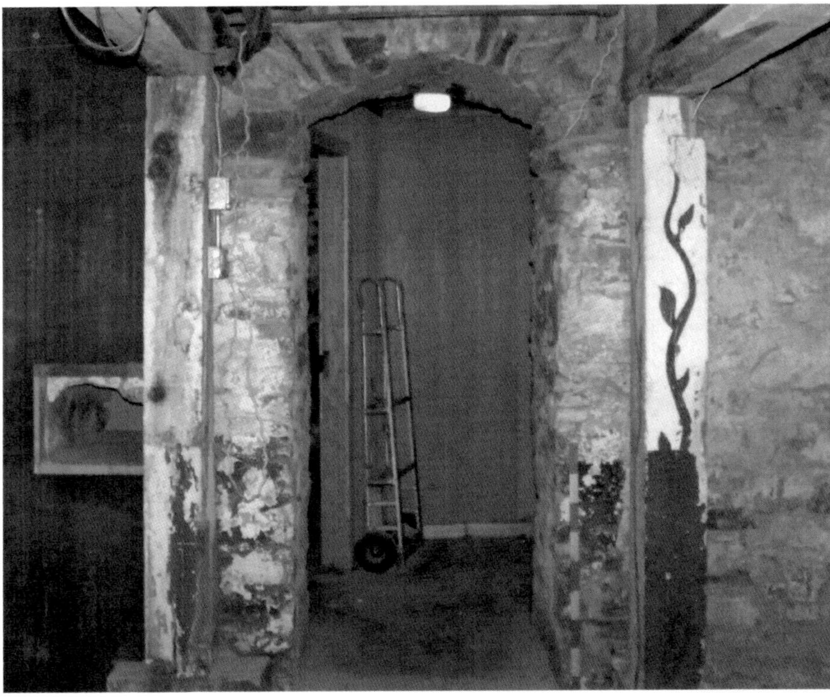

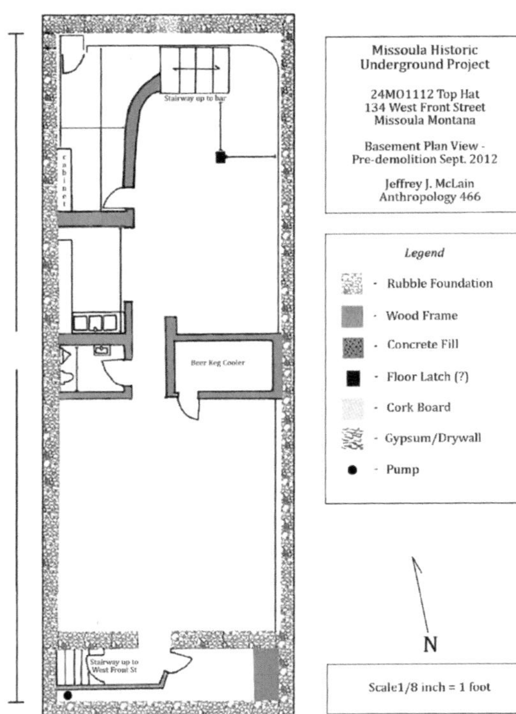

Above: Cobble and brick archway in the basement of the Top Hat that provides access between the basement and the sidewalk void. *Photo by Lisa Menery.*

Right: Plan map of the Top Hat basement and sidewalk void. *Map by Jeff McLain.*

that once opened a hidden door in the north wall during Prohibition.[39] The door, she said, was now covered by drywall. The encasement was recorded as Feature 1. The latch was no longer inside the encasement, and electricians confirmed that the encasement did not appear to be connected to anything under the floor. Thus, our investigations were unable to confirm whether the latch actually opened a secret door.

Feature 2 was the arched stone doorway between the basement and the sidewalk void. There are wooden pegs embedded in the stone on both sides of the doorway that appear to be either remnants of a wooden door over the archway or possibly support pegs for when the archway was constructed. The sidewalk void itself, constructed of stone rubble masonry, was documented as Feature 3. In the southeast corner of the void was a Pomona turbine pump located directly below a manhole in the sidewalk above.

Soon after the mapping and feature recording work were completed, demolition began for renovations to modernize the basement and to add a kitchen. Demolition of the drywall failed to uncover the suspected Prohibition-era door that would have been operated by the floor latch. It did, however, uncover a door under the stairs, approximately dead center in the basement's north-facing wall, which measured twenty-six feet and ten inches. This was a wooden door with sheet metal attached to the other side. It swung outward, so it was not opened until the earth on the other side was excavated. Due to the construction, we were not able to record this door as a feature, but the location of it on the wall inside was noted on the basement plan map. It is still undetermined whether the floor latch ever operated this door. The recent modifications to the building removed all opportunities to further investigate this.

Incidentally, the mapping of this basement and the discovery of the wooden door completely justified the significance of documenting basement spaces in the downtown Missoula historic district. When the plan map of the Top Hat basement was overlaid with the 1888 Sanborn map, the location of the wooden door discovered during demolition clearly lines up with the door of the "underground liquor cellar" noted on the Sanborn map. When the dirt was excavated in the rear of the building with a bulldozer, no underground room or cellar was discovered. The stratigraphy suggested that it had likely been demolished and the area filled in earlier, possibly even by 1893, when the Sanborn maps cease to document this cellar. No artifact recovery was performed at this property, although during the outside ground excavation, some artifacts were recovered by the construction company and given to the owner.

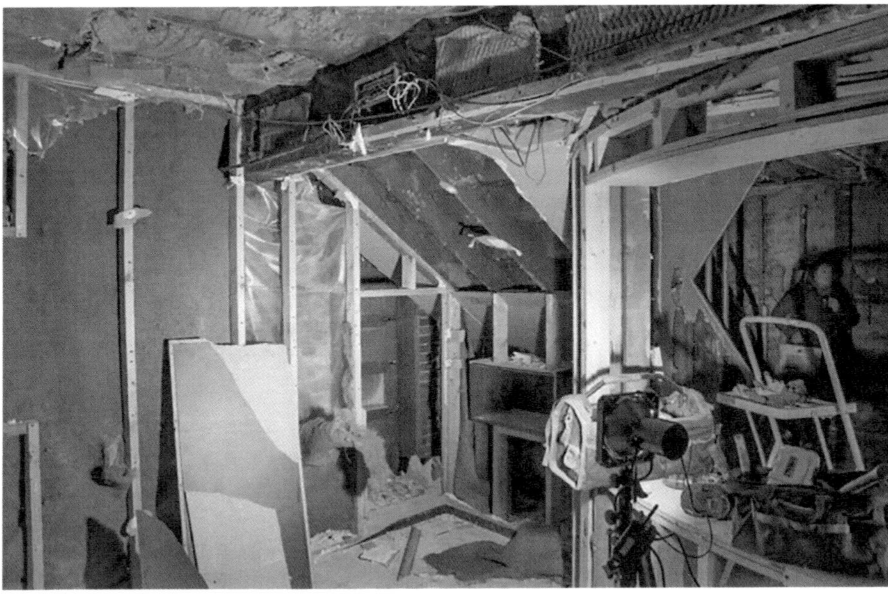

A door found under the stairs during basement demolition in the Top Hat. *Photo by Jeff McLain.*

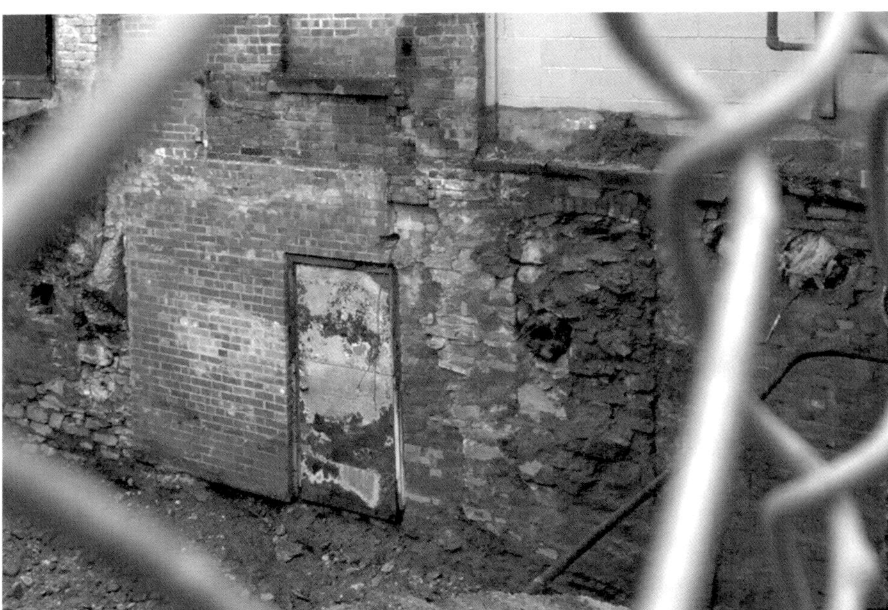

The same door under the stairs in the basement of the Top Hat from the exterior after excavation of the ground in rear of building. *Author's collection.*

Summary Analysis

With the exception of approximately a 10-year period as an auto garage/ auto sales business during Prohibition, the main floor of the building on this property has consistently served as a public drinking establishment during its nearly 130 years of existence. The underground spaces have been used for a variety of purposes. The basement most recently has been used for storage and a staging area for live bands. The finished bathroom, cold storage locker and workbench are suggestive of such use.

The sidewalk void is rather small and houses mechanical equipment and the turbine pump thus suggesting utility purposes again, much like parts of the Hammond sidewalk voids. The brick archway into the basement with the remnants of wood in the brick could either suggest temporary supports for the wall while the archway was built or possibly the existence at one time of a door blocking the sidewalk void from the rest of the basement.

The north doorway that was uncovered when renovations began, particularly given the fact that it lined up perfectly with the once general merchandise and then underground liquor cellar area, is an exciting architectural feature, yet given the time period of the late 1880s, underground liquor storage was not necessarily a nefarious activity. This property had no access to the steam tunnel system. The oral history about a secret Prohibition-era door and the ability for cars to enter and exit the basement while it was an auto shop fuel other theories about Prohibition-era underground use. These were unfortunately outside the time period and scope at this stage of research.

Much like the Hammond Building/Arcade, nothing suggests connection with the Chinese community. The few artifacts recovered by the contractors during excavation of the back lot appear to have been associated with a blacksmith shop that was at one time located next door.

MacKenzie River Pizza Company

This property is a one-story commercial structure. The foundation is made of concrete and stone. Although the building was remodeled in 1972, it retains some of the original design and materials. This factor and the building's location make it a contributing property to the downtown historic district. The front entrance of the building faces north to West Front Street, whereas the south (rear) side of the building faces the Clark Fork River.

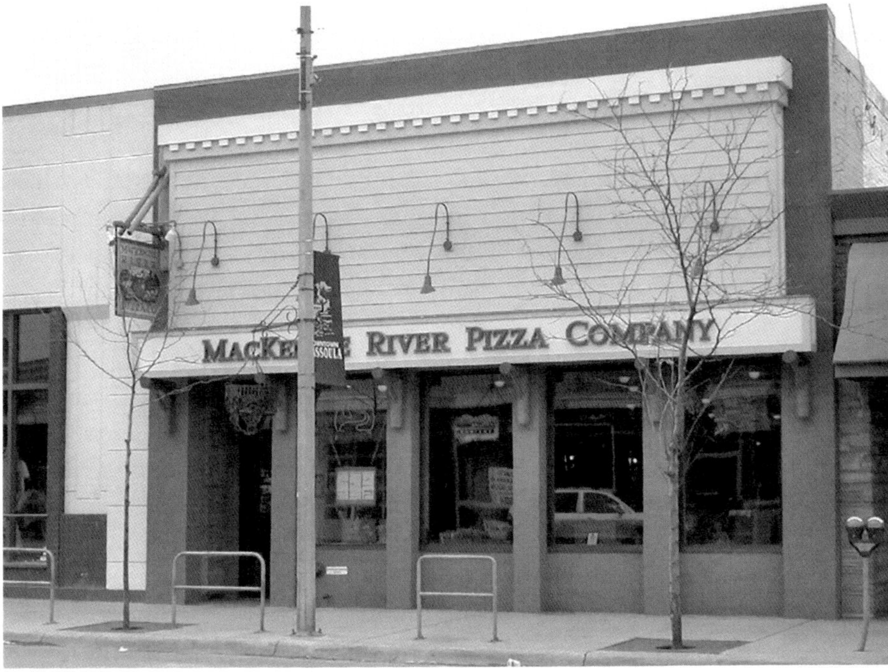

MacKenzie River Pizza Company, located at 137 West Front Street. *Photo from the 2005 Montana Historical and Architectural Inventory.*

Historical Background

This property was chosen not only because the owner was in contact early with the Missoula Historic Underground Project team about a mysterious closet in his basement office but also because early historical research showed that a Chinese restaurant had operated at that location during the early twentieth century. This was interesting for two reasons. First and foremost, given the local lore and research question, this property had the potential to answer some specific questions about Chinese American life and business in Missoula. Second, it was curious that this Chinese restaurant was closer to the center of the powerful Front and Higgins intersection than to the Chinatown area of West Front Street that was concentrated farther to the west.

The earliest Sanborn record for this space (1884) shows that there was a vacant saloon at this address. While it likely was not vacant for very long given Missoula's propensity for saloons and given the relative abundance of saloons along Front Street during the late nineteenth and early twentieth centuries, no evidence was found for what else might have been there between 1884 and the next Sanborn map for that area in 1888. In addition, this building and a few others next to it likely burned shortly before the 1888 Sanborn was created because the Sanborn for this year shows ruins in this lot and empty lots to either side of it. This site remained vacant until 1891 when the lot was occupied by a loan office, a saloon and a restaurant. Generally during this time, Chinese-operated businesses were labeled as "Chinese" on Sanborn maps so it is likely that the restaurant shown this early is not the Chinese restaurant referenced earlier.

The first mention of a restaurant on this lot being Chinese-operated is on the 1902 Sanborn map, which reads "Chine Rest." The Polk Directory entry for this address in 1903 lists a restaurant run by Samuel Yontz. It is thought that this could be an incorrect spelling of the same name, Sam Yung, listed as having the restaurant only two years later.[40] At times his name is also spelled as "Young" and "Yong." From 1907 to 1912 Sam's name disappears. In 1909, the space became a Japanese cigar shop and then a barbershop before Sam Yung returned and opened a new restaurant in a presumably new building in 1912.

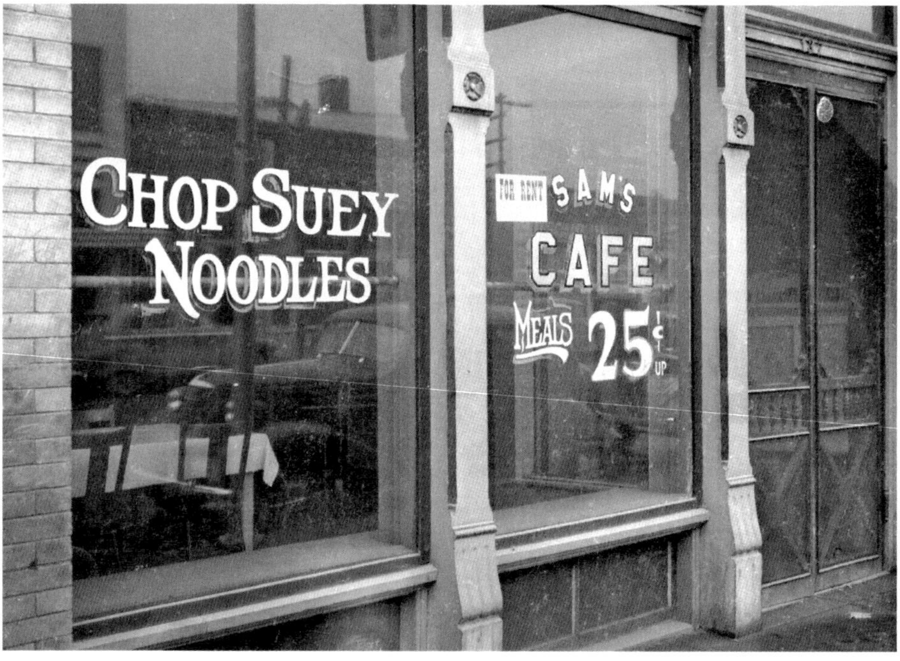

Sam Yung's Café, circa 1940. *Photo No. 90.1131, Archives and Special Collections, Mansfield Library, University of Montana.*

The *Missoulian* newspaper printed an article on March 31, 1912, about Sam Yung returning to Missoula after a lengthy visit to his hometown in Canton (Guangdong), China. He had returned to start a new restaurant that would open the following day. The Sanborn map for 1912 shows a larger restaurant at this location. Curiously, it does not label it as specifically Chinese, at least not until 1921. Sam is listed as the proprietor in the Polk Directory until 1929, when Ham Tong is listed as proprietor for one year; this could be another misspelling of Sam Yung or Yong. Dirk Yue took over in 1930 and operated the restaurant until it went out of business in 1943. It remained Sam's Café until then, even without Sam.

Archaeological Survey

Turning to the basement and the archaeological survey conducted at this property, the primary focus became the mystery closet in the sidewalk void on the north side of the building's basement. The basement closet is situated in the northeast corner of the basement in the restaurant manager's office. Inside the closet is an intact arched brick doorway that has been blocked with cement cinder blocks representative of the work performed in the 1980s on many sidewalk voids in the downtown area. Casual conversation with a patron named "Roscoe" at the Top Hat across the street one evening led to a discussion of the project and the story from him that this sidewalk void was once an opium den. The Sullivan sidewalk report does show a small sidewalk void on the other side of the blocked doorway; however, it is also one of the very small voids in the downtown at three feet, six inches in width and eight feet, four inches in depth. The report also suggested that it was no longer used space and that it should just be closed. According to the steam tunnel map, there are no known steam pipes or links to the steam tunnel in this area.

This is another basement where operations of the current restaurant business prevented a plan map of the entire basement. The doorway in the closet was recorded as the only feature at this site. It was noted during the feature recording that the cinder blocks did not extend all the way to the floor of the closet. There is instead a sizeable debris deposit of dirt fill, coal fragments, shredded newspaper, mortar and red brick fragments at the base of the arched doorway. It appears that the cinder blocks were just placed on top of the debris and built up from there.

The restaurant management allowed a small-scale test excavation to screen the debris for artifacts. All of the material on top of the dried cement

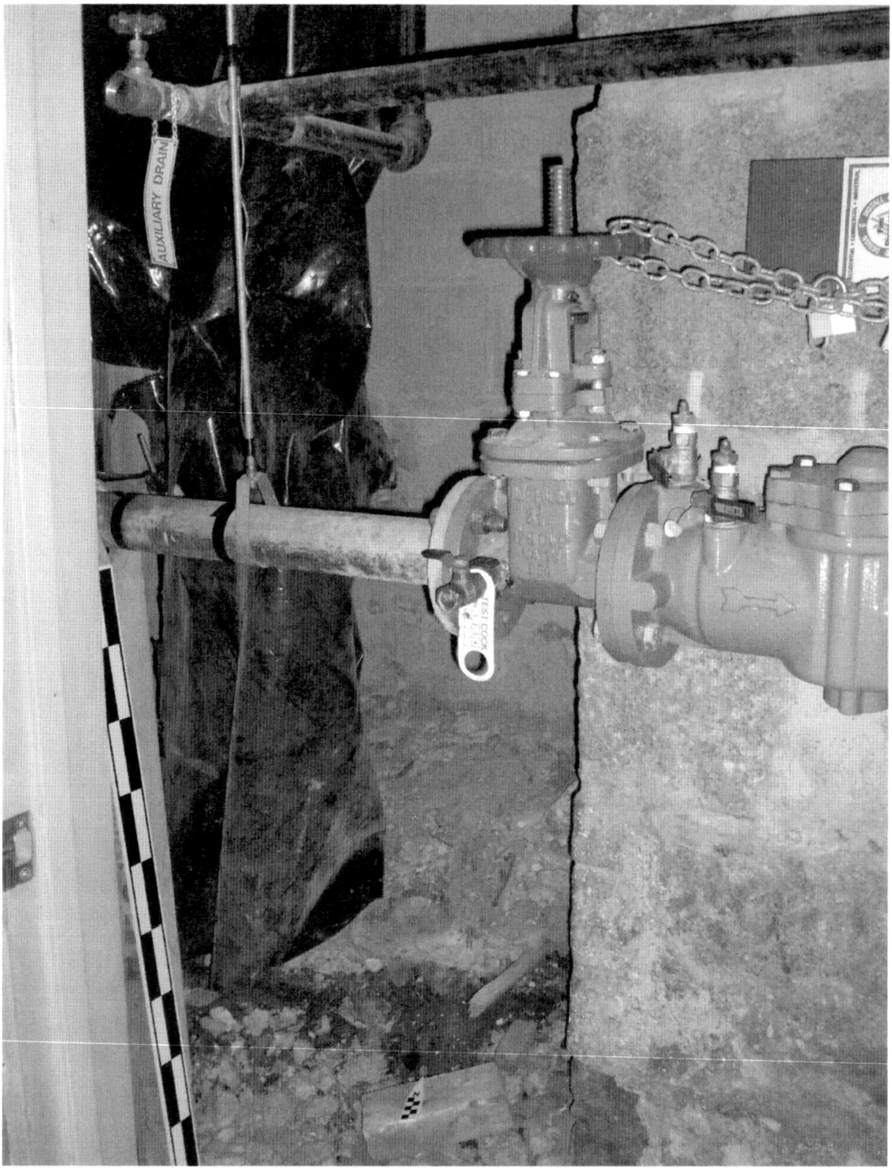

MacKenzie River Pizza Company closet leading to the sidewalk void with the visible cinder block wall and debris/fill at the base of the wall. *Photo by Mary Bobbitt.*

flow was labeled "Level 1." Due to the unevenness, looseness of the debris and the tight space of the closet, neat removal was difficult so this material that basically fell away was labeled "Level 1 Clean-up." It was discovered during

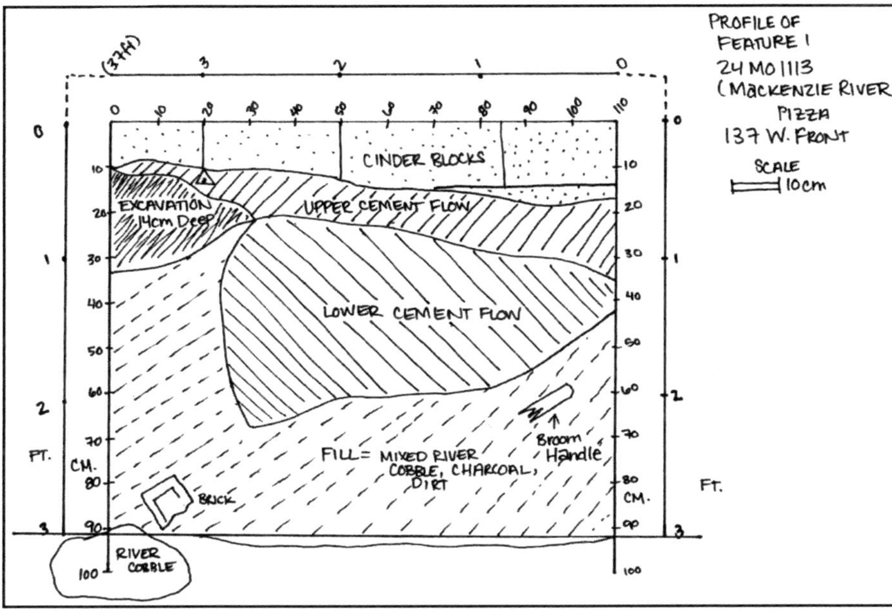

Profile map of the MacKenzie River Pizza Company closet. *Map by Ryan Dudgeon.*

the excavation that it was quite possible to excavate into the void through a cavity under the cinder blocks. The profile map (viewing the space from the side) highlights these details. At this point, the excavation was stopped to determine whether this would prove fruitful and would also be safe.

When the buckets were screened, most of the artifacts appeared to be relatively modern (i.e., 1980s soda bottle caps and strips of newspaper dated to the 1960s). Due to the modern nature of the artifacts and concern over structural integrity of the sidewalk above, it was determined that further excavation would likely not yield any additional pertinent information at the time and should be halted. Acquiring the necessary permissions and taking into account safety precautions, it is suggested that possible further excavation be conducted to see what, if anything, remains inside the void itself.

Summary Analysis

This building's history of being Sam Yung's restaurant is interesting for three reasons. First of all, Sam's restaurant was located in the busy and "respectable" section of the 100 block of West Front Street. He was not located in what was then Missoula's Chinatown. Second, the restaurant was in business for at least thirty-one years and well past the time that the majority of the Chinese community had left Missoula. Third, Sam appears to have been well liked and respected in the community based on the March 31, 1912 *Missoulian* article. Unable to find any other information in city records about Sam Yung or his restaurant, it is unknown why this would have been the case, but it appears he likely had a different experience than many others in the Missoula Chinese community or that of the Chinese in the American West.[41]

Most attention was focused on the closet that contained the sidewalk void entrance. Working with the oral history that the sidewalk void was once an opium den and knowing that it was the location of a Chinese restaurant, interest was piqued to find any material record of there ever being such a thing associated with this basement/sidewalk void. Although the property was for many years a Chinese establishment, there appears to be no archaeological signature in that basement to speak of.

Unfortunately, not being able to access the actual sidewalk void, it is unknown whether any material record of the Chinese restaurant still remains inside. The size of the sidewalk void, however, implies that it is unlikely this space would have been used as an opium den as local lore suggests. The sidewalk void is merely three and a half feet wide and less than eight and a half feet deep—the smallest found so far. Spaces for smoking opium would traditionally have been larger than this sidewalk void due to the need for lounging and relaxing, often in bunk-style beds.[42] The artifacts that were recovered in the small-scale test excavation revealed all modern debris (primarily circa 1980 material), probably from the 1981 fill project.

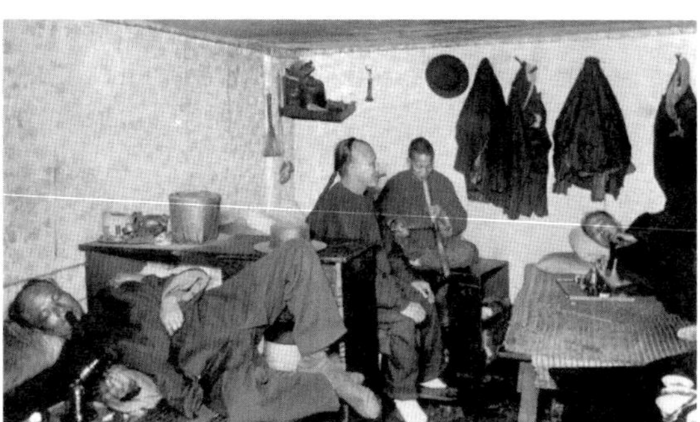

Photo of an opium den from between 1890 and 1910. *Photo from the Library of Congress, LC-D418-30816.*

Montgomery Distillery

This property is immediately east of and adjacent to the property associated with the MacKenzie River Pizza Company. From approximately 1890 to 1902, the building was known as the Schilling Block. It burned on February 20, 1926, and the lot was razed by the following September. It was rebuilt sometime around 1932, but the basement/foundation appears to be original and shows signs of fire, such as smoke damage on the masonry. The present business that occupies this building, the Montgomery Distillery, follows a long tradition of the Schilling Block's role in the alcohol trade.

Historical Background

According to the 1884 Sanborn map, an adobe-style building existed on this lot and served as a saloon and chophouse, a type of restaurant. By 1888, the

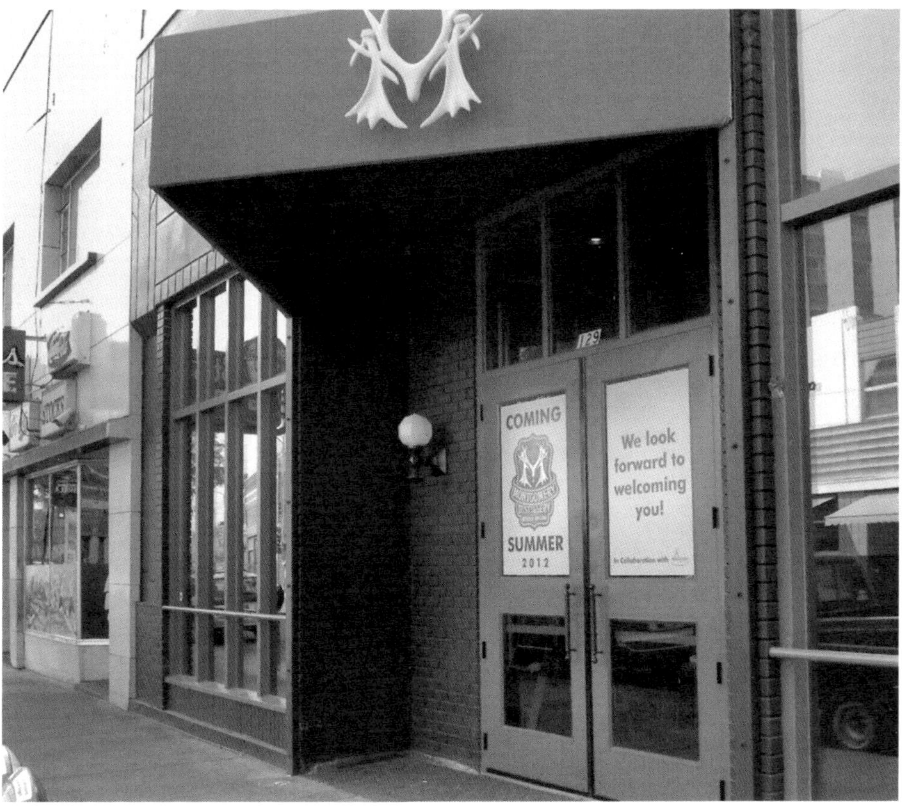

Montgomery Distillery at 129 West Front Street. *Photo by Mark Gibbons Jr.*

map depicts "adobe ruins" of a fire. It appears the fire destroyed quite a few buildings in that area, including the vacant saloon next door that became Sam Yung's restaurant. The Schilling Block was erected circa 1889. This building is easily discernible on the Sanborn maps, not only being labeled as the Schilling Block but also because of the distinctive bay window on the second floor. It housed a tailor shop, liquors and cigars, lodging on the second floor and a saloon in the basement. It consistently served as a lodging business with a saloon until the era of Prohibition, when the structure/block became the Motor Company Garage with a capacity of eighteen cars, according to the 1921 Sanborn map; this appears to be part of a pattern observed on the Sanborn maps from the 1920s in that many saloon spaces in Missoula seem to transition to businesses associated with the auto industry.

The 1891 Sanborn map shows two separate basement saloons, with one on either side of a dividing wall. The sidewalk entrances shown in the Sullivan Report likely accessed these saloon establishments.[43] There was also a shooting gallery in the basement (in the saloon on the west side of the building), and according to the Missoula Fire Department scrapbook there was a fire in the basement shooting gallery in 1901.[44] The two internal doorways still provide passage between the basement and the void. This evidence suggests that the sidewalk void and at least parts of the basement are original to the 1889 building. There are neither steam pipes nor any access to the steam tunnel system from this basement.

Archaeological Survey

During the first stage of the study, it was once again fortunate that this was another space under new ownership and renovations. Thanks to the building owners, our crews were given access to create a plan map of the basement and sidewalk void space. The plan map that was created and the Sullivan sidewalk report drawing are quite similar, suggesting that the void is the same as it was in 1981.

Six features were recorded for this property. Feature 1 is a possible coal chute or other type of furnace access. The metal door is twelve inches by twelve inches in the west wall. There is brick around the door and stone masonry around that. Inside the door there appears to be burned wood and brick. Being that the door is in the adjoining wall with MacKenzie River Pizza and there is another similar door on that side, it is believed that the two properties may have connected at some point, at least shared a coal chute.

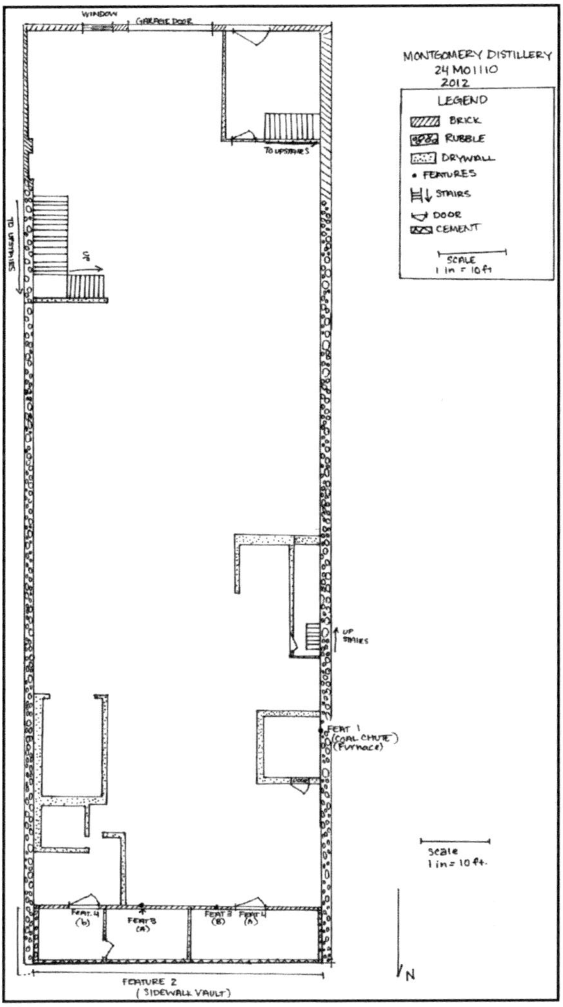

Plan map of the Montgomery Distillery basement and sidewalk void. *Map by Ryan Dudgeon.*

The sidewalk void as a whole was recorded as Feature 2. The length of the void east to west is forty feet, four inches with a width of eight feet, eight inches. The south (building-side) wall is brick with two arched brick doorways and two inverted arches set into the wall that resemble a flattened "U" shape. Inverted arches were used in the foundation walls of buildings to distribute the load, and in the early 1890s, when the Schilling Block would have been built, they were used to "take up less vertical space than a spread footing" and provide stronger structural support. It is likely that the unique arches in the Schilling Block's sidewalk void represent such structural support.[45]

The east and west walls are stone masonry, and the north (street-side) wall is concrete. The stone and brick walls are noticeably blackened by fire, providing further evidence that the sidewalk void walls predate the 1925 fire. Features 3 and 4 are the inverted arches in the south wall of the sidewalk void. Feature 3 is in the east side of the void and measures six feet, two inches long, twenty-two inches from top to bottom and six feet, two inches off the ground. Feature 4 in the west side measures five feet, four inches long. It is also twenty-two inches from top to bottom but measures six feet, four inches off the ground. Features 5 (east side) and 6 (west side) are the original doorway arches above the current modern doors.

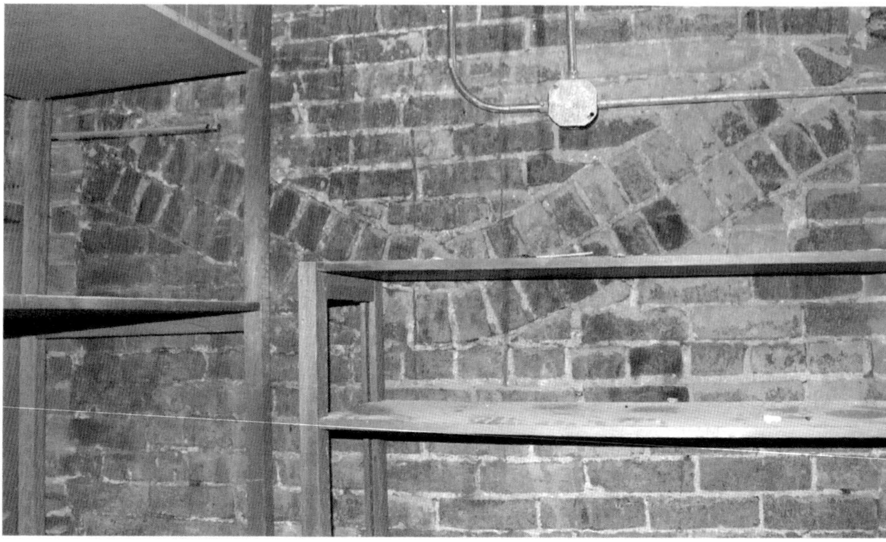

One of two inverted arches in the Montgomery Distillery sidewalk void. *Photo by Jada Molton.*

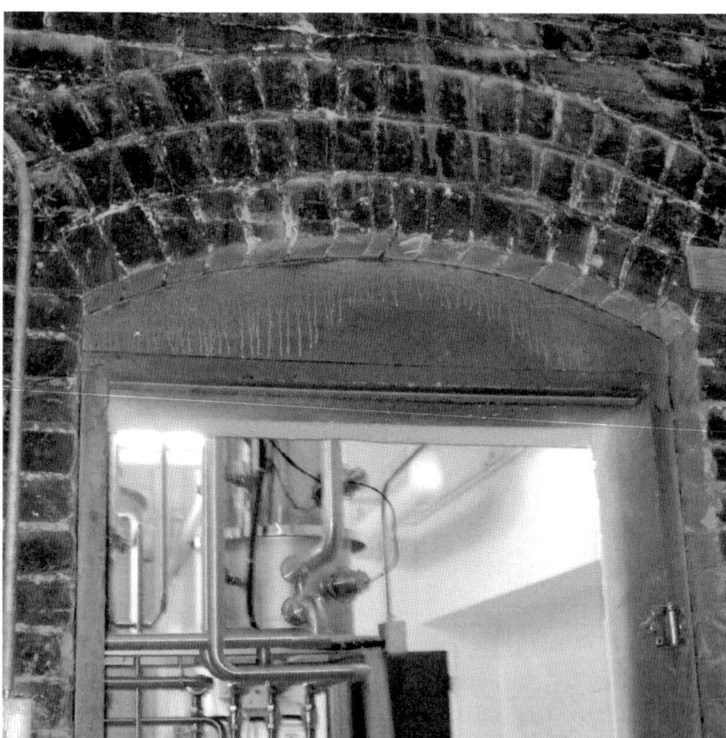

Brick archway connecting the basement and the sidewalk void in the Montgomery Distillery. *Author's collection.*

Summary Analysis

The basement and sidewalk voids for this property appear to date to approximately 1889. At that time, there were a number of businesses in the structure above ground—a tailor, a liquor and cigar store, lodging and a saloon. According to the information gathered, there were two saloons and a shooting gallery—all located in the basement and accessed by the dual sidewalk void entrances. During the Prohibition era, the structure ceased providing public drinking services and turned into an auto garage with a capacity of eighteen cars, some of which would have needed to be located in the basement, likely through the still existing garage door access on the south (rear) wall. There does not appear to be any steam pipe conduits or tunnel access. No evidence associated with this property suggests connections to the Chinese community except for neighboring Sam Yung.

Piece of Mind

The building that includes the Piece of Mind shop on the first floor and apartments on the second is actually considered to be 123, 125 and 127

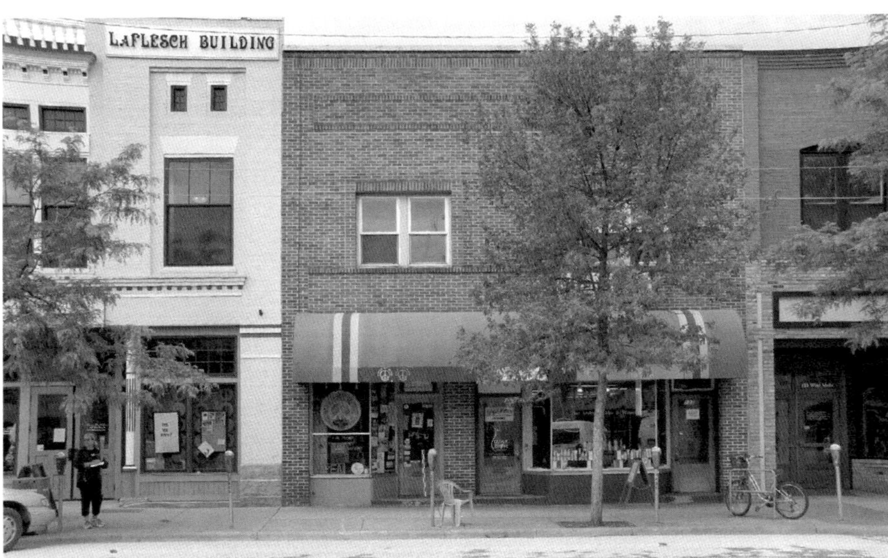

Piece of Mind at 123 West Main Street. *Photo by Bethany Hauer.*

West Main Street today. It is a two-story brick commercial structure. The basement is oddly shaped and divided into four sections, all of which seemed to have been built at a different time from one another. Except for a small area at the bottom of the stairs, the basement is dark, lit by a single bulb with a pull string in the open-rafter ceiling.

Historical Background

A 1958 *Missoulian* newspaper article states that at one time the southern section (in the rear of the building) of the basement was a Chinese restaurant, except that at the time, it was not below ground. The article explains that the restaurant was set back approximately seventy-five feet from the street and was situated in a ravine. "In about 1886," the ravine was filled to bring that area up to street grade, burying the restaurant and turning it into a basement when a building was erected over it. Later additions to the building brought the building forward closer to the street. Despite these details in the 1958 article, research in the 1886 newspaper and the city council meeting minutes from the same time frame did not turn up any information about the ravine-filling project. The ravine, according to the article, ran southwest to the river from Main Street through the west end of the 100 block of West Front Street.

Curiously, the Sanborn maps never show a Chinese restaurant in that location; rather, a meat market shows up on the 1890 Sanborn. The 1890 building is two stories in front and one in the back and is likely the same building that is there today. No records or maps have ever been found that support information about a ravine being there at any point.

This building did have a sidewalk void at one time, but it had already been filled in prior to the 1981 Sullivan sidewalk report.[46] There is clear evidence in the basement of two steps up to a doorway that would have led to the sidewalk void, but there are no visible or documented details as to the size of the void. There was no access to it from the sidewalk above, only through the doorway in the basement. There are no steam pipes or steam tunnel access for this building on the city steam tunnel map.

Archaeological Survey

The owner of this property, Jim Caras, being aware of the Missoula Historic Underground Project through an article in the *Missoulian*

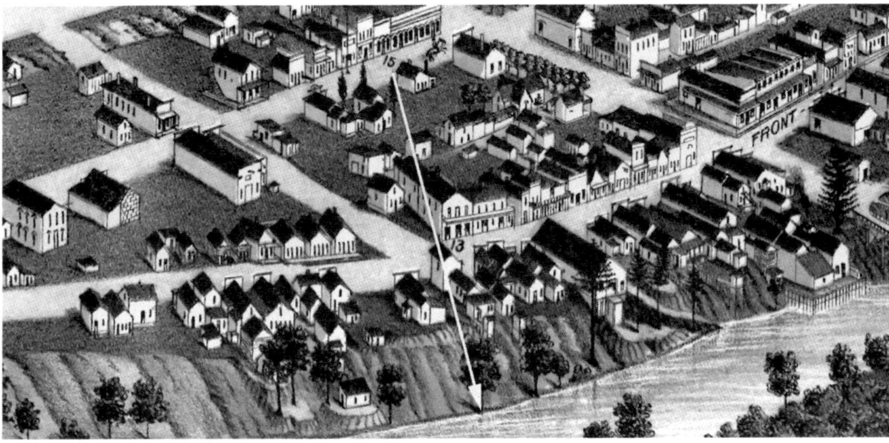

Bird's-eye view map of Missoula looking northeast, 1884. The arrow indicates approximately where the reported ravine would have been according to the 1958 *Missoulian*. *Illustration courtesy of the Library of Congress Bird's-Eye View Maps collection.*

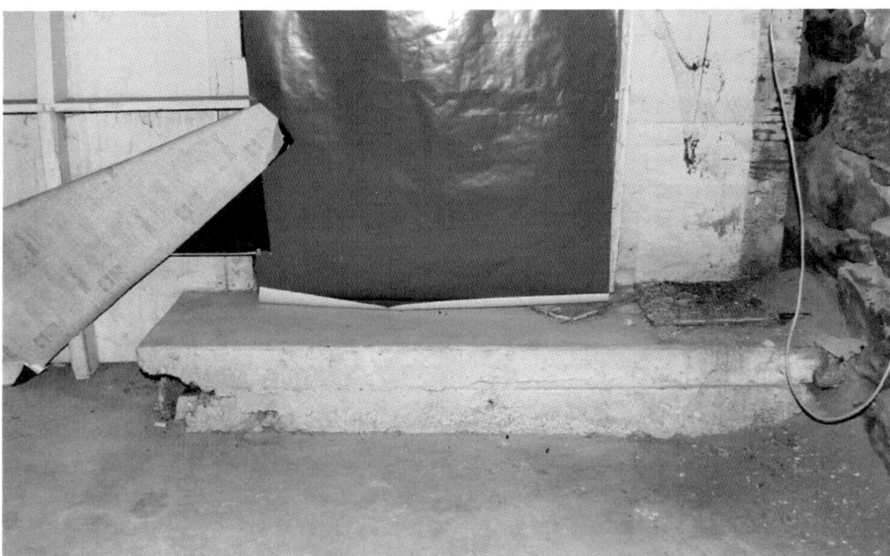

A step up into the now sealed and likely in-filled sidewalk void. *Photo by Bethany Hauer.*

newspaper, contacted us to see if we were interested in examining some graffiti on the wall under the stairs to the basement. The writing was in Chinese, perhaps some Japanese and also some English. There were remnants of a Chinese banner on the wall. Of all the properties examined,

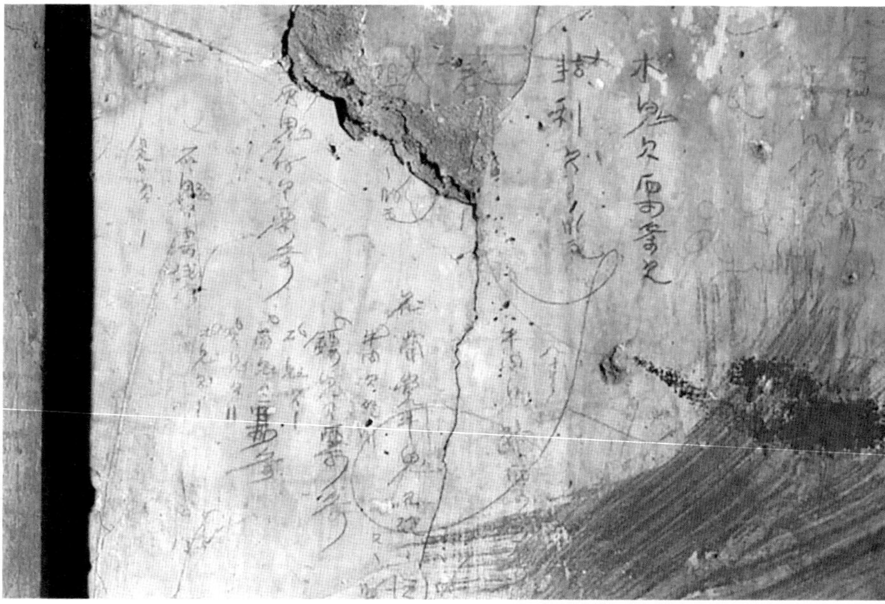

Chinese, English and perhaps Japanese writing on the wall in the Piece of Mind basement. *Author's collection.*

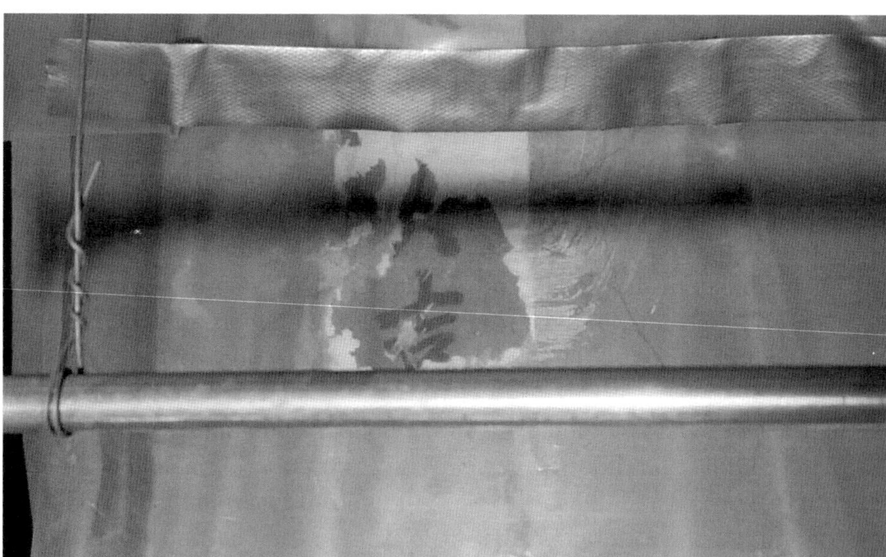

Remnant of Chinese New Year banner in basement of Piece of Mind. *Photo by Bethany Hauer.*

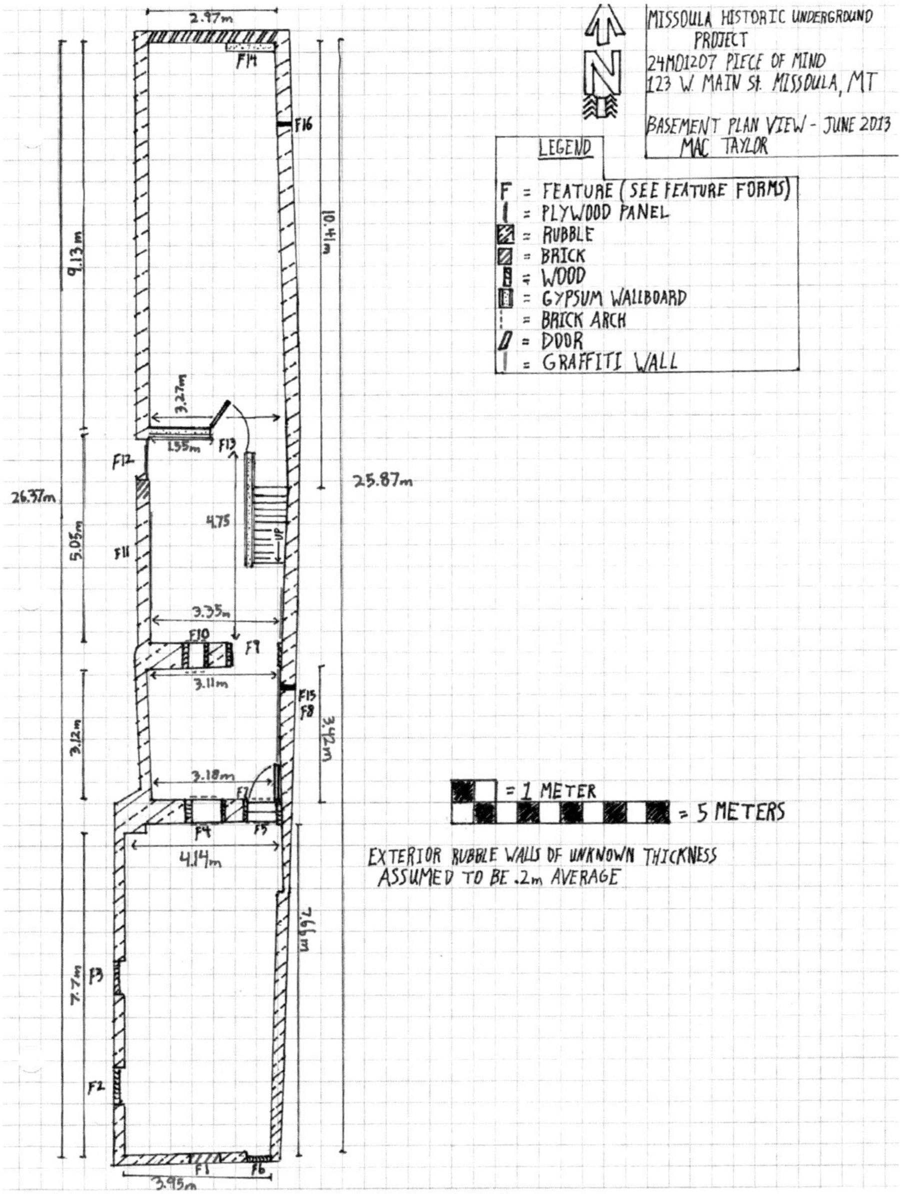

Plan map of the awkwardly shaped basement of Piece of Mind. *Map by Mac Taylor.*

this appears to be the only one with an underground archaeological signature of the Chinese.

The basement for this property is so awkwardly shaped that acquiring accurate measurements was challenging, but the crew produced a plan map for this space. There is another discrepancy worth mentioning when comparing the 1958 *Missoulian* article with the map findings: the article states that the original building that was buried by filling in the ravine was set approximately seventy-five feet back from the street. Two sections of the basement that are closest to the street appear to be of newer construction based on drywall and paint, leading to the belief that the two rear rooms or even the farthest south room were part of the original building. Once the map was completed, the measurements taken to create the plan map do not support that the original building was set back that far from the street. Even taking into consideration wall thickness and margin of error in original building measurements or the ones we took, the seventy-five-foot measurement just does not add up, further contradicting the facts in the 1958 *Missoulian* article.

There were sixteen features recorded at this property. These are all identified on the plan map. Features of importance to note are the bricked-in underground door in the south wall (Feature 1) and boarded-up windows in the west wall (Features 2 and 3), which is an adjoining wall with the business next door. While two separate businesses appear on the 1890 Sanborn map, the building was clearly erected as one building. This makes the windows on the west wall even more perplexing because they would have looked into the

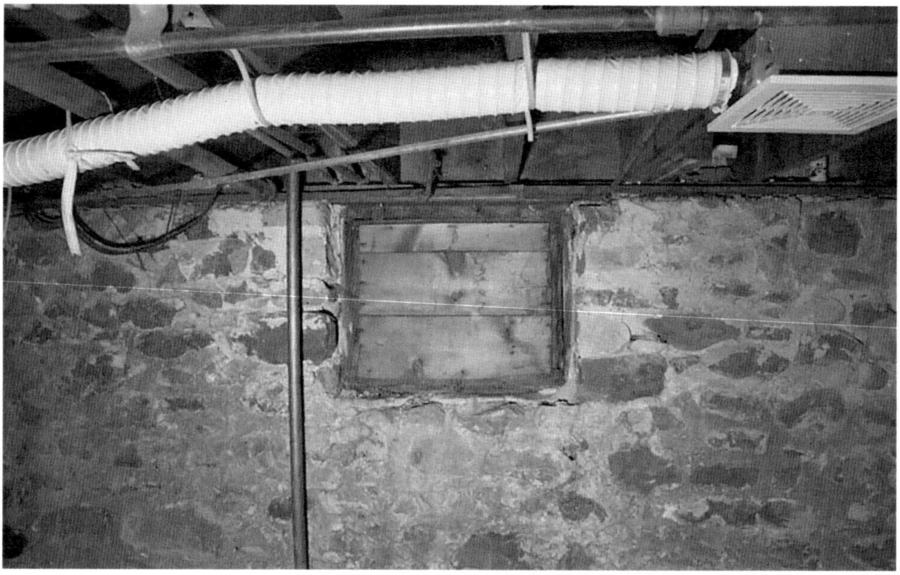

Feature 2 in the Piece of Mind basement is one of two windows in the west wall, which is also a shared wall with the business next door. *Author's collection.*

basement next door. At some point a doorway was made to connect the two basements as well (Feature 12). The line on the map points specifically to where the graffiti wall is located (Feature 8).

There are other interior doors and windows, also giving the appearance of separate construction times. For ease of reference, the rooms are numbered, from south to north, 1–4. There are a window and a door between Rooms 1 and 2. Although the door has a wooden frame and a wood/glass combination door, there is a brick archway in which the door was placed (Feature 5). In Room 2, on the wall between the door and window, is the remnant of a red and black Chinese banner.

There is another doorway with a brick archway but no door between Room 2 and 3, as well as another internal window beside the doorway. There is one more door between Rooms 3 and 4 made of wood with glass panes.

Summary Analysis

This property became the biggest mystery of the entire project. It was, of course, chosen for the interesting wall of graffiti—both in Chinese and English and possibly even Japanese. The most intriguing aspect of this property in terms of the underground narrative is the common belief that it was once a Chinese restaurant set in a ravine that was buried when the ravine was filled. This is said to have made the above-ground structure into a basement on which two stories were later built. Based on the 1958 article, this could make sense, yet there are a number of problems with this report based on the data acquired during this study.

The most glaring issue is that, at least according to the Sanborn maps and Polk Directory research, the property was never a Chinese restaurant. Thus far, no other property record or deed search has been able to confirm that there was ever a Chinese restaurant in this location either. Additionally, the Sanborn maps show that when the ravine would have been filled in 1886, it was actually an empty lot. An extensive search in the newspaper as well as city council meeting minutes do not reveal any information about the filling of a large ravine that ran from the building's location on West Main Street south and all the way to the river. This would have cut through the end of the 100 block of West Front Street on both the north and south sides of the street, and no evidence supports this ever happening. Based on readings of the city council meeting minutes from this time period and the mundane things they discussed, one could easily assume that this would have been a major project and recorded.

Also according to the 1958 *Missoulian* article, the original building that is now the oldest section of the basement was set back seventy-five feet from the street. The measurements and mapping, even allowing for a margin of error, do not support this assertion. The burying of the building to create a basement also does not explain the windows in the west wall. The current business west of and adjacent to this property is all the same structure. They share a common wall with the west-facing windows in the Piece of Mind basement as part of that wall. The windows were not external. The east Piece of Mind wall is shared with the west wall of the LaFlesch building. Even though the LaFlesch building was constructed approximately ten years after the Piece of Mind property was built, the first-floor west wall of the LaFlesch building shows a different pattern of brick in the exact space with the same dimensions above the Piece of Mind graffiti wall in the basement next door. This suggests that these two buildings were connected as well, with the different brick pattern on the first floor of the LaFlesch building having once been an opening to Piece of Mind.

The most perplexing discrepancy between the historical record and the data recovered during this project is the translation of the graffiti. Six different Chinese-speaking people were contacted in an attempt to translate the Chinese characters. The consensus was that the writing was somehow different from traditional Chinese writing, possibly a form of shorthand. The ages of the individuals asked to translate ranged from thirty-five to eighty-five to take generational differences into account. Of the characters that were legible, the translations suggested anything from "waking up late on a Tuesday," "ticket," "wood" and "cow or ox" to more ominous words/phrases such as "ghost or monster" that appears multiple times and a phrase about "praying at night."

Cow or ox could refer to the meat market that once occupied the building. Perhaps it was Chinese-owned even though the Sanborn maps do not specify this. The reference to cow/ox could also refer to the Chinese zodiac for Year of the Ox (1877, 1889, 1901, 1913, 1925, 1937…). The character for "ghost" could have a supernatural connotation or could mean "white people" since "ghost" was a common word that Chinese immigrants used to refer to someone non-Chinese.[47]

The south side of the 100 block of West Main Street where this property is located purportedly served as an area for Chinese brothels in the basements, connected through adjoining sidewalk voids.[48] The engineering report for this block of sidewalk voids is inconclusive as to whether these buildings had connecting sidewalk voids. This bit of oral history regarding specifically Chinese brothels in a basement is at the very heart of our hypothesis. Despite the existence of Chinese graffiti, the research does not even support this property being associated with the Chinese community. Since the research does not disprove it either, it is possible to understand how the folklore about a Chinese brothel in the basement could originate, develop and become part of the collective memory in Missoula.

The LaFlesch Building

The LaFlesch Building, also known as the Loft and the Downtown Dance Collective, is immediately east of and adjacent to Piece of Mind. As a matter

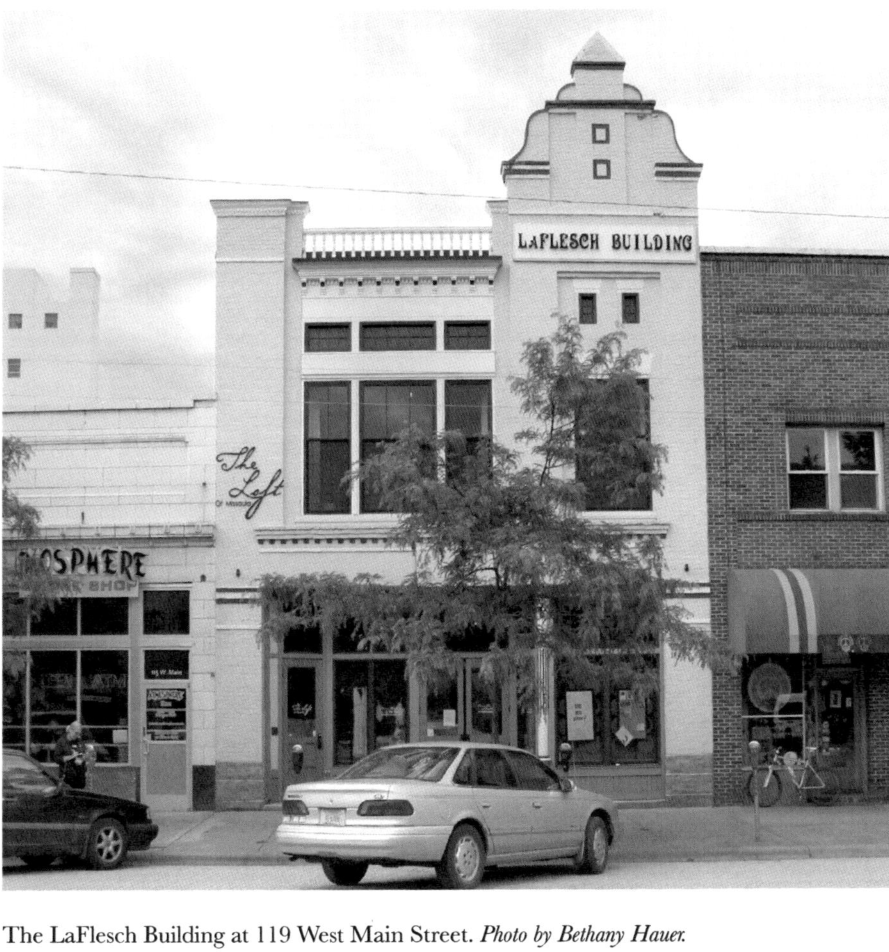

The LaFlesch Building at 119 West Main Street. *Photo by Bethany Hauer.*

of fact, the two share a common wall, as noted before, making it possible to talk and pass items through the spaces where stovepipes were once attached. The present owner, Jay LaFlesch, having done a lot of historical research already and being interested in the underground project, came forward and offered the space for our survey.

Historical Background

After speaking with Mr. LaFlesch at length about what he knew of the history of the building, the crew learned that this building was once the offices of the *Missoula Gazette*. The *Missoula Gazette* was started by A.B. Hammond—the same Hammond who built the original Hammond Building and the Missoula Mercantile. Mr. Hammond was displeased with the picture painted of him by the *Missoulian* newspaper and so began his own news source until he was able to purchase the *Missoulian* outright. The *Missoula Gazette* was somewhat short-lived in comparison, and this building actually became the *Missoulian* headquarters by 1902.

The building was erected circa 1890–91, according to the Sanborn maps. It was a two-story masonry brick commercial structure with a flat roof and a parapet. At some point the building façade was covered with black glass panels, and the second-story façade was covered with various brickwork styles. In 2005, the building went under extensive renovation by Mr. LaFlesch to restore it to the original historic character and won a Missoula Historic Preservation award for exemplary restoration.

According to the 1884 Sanborn map, there were two small wooden structures in this space that served as the printing office for the *Weekly Missoulian*. By the 1888 map, these two buildings were sitting vacant, and the *Missoulian* had moved across the street and occupied a space that is now a city parking garage. Around 1888–90, one of the small buildings became a restaurant and the other a Chinese store. By 1891, those two structures were gone, and in their place the building now known as the LaFlesch building was erected. There was water-powered printing in the basement, presumably for Hammond's *Gazette*, and a saloon and offices on the first floor. There were likely lodgings on the second floor.

The building became the *Missoulian* newspaper complex between 1893 and 1902, with printing still in the basement and all other departments of the newspaper in the same building. By 1912, the building was occupied by a meat market or warehouse since the *Missoulian* moved a few doors to the

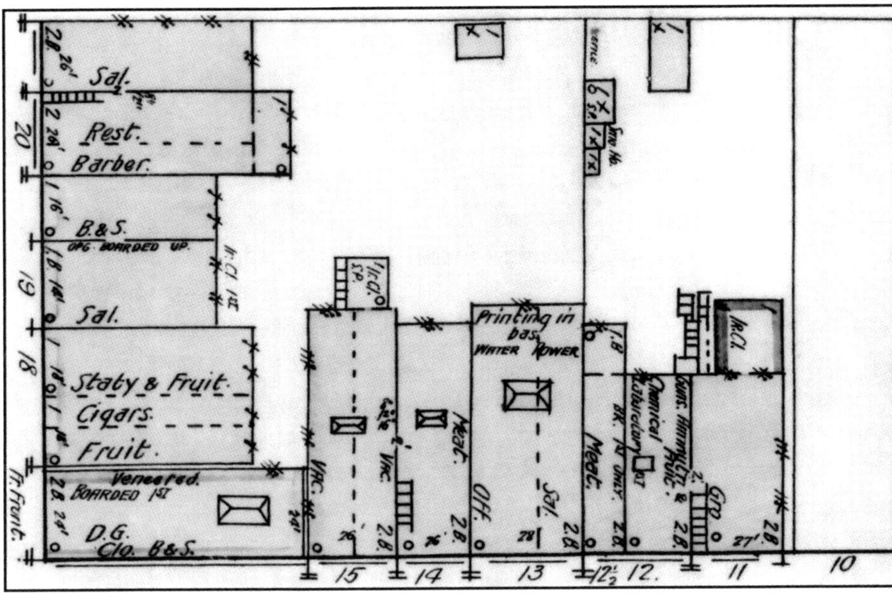

An 1891 Sanborn Fire Insurance Map for 119 West Main Street. *Map used with permission from Environmental Data Resources Inc.*

east to 131 West Main Street, the other side of the Piece of Mind building. In 1921, a store and refrigeration plant occupied the building, with the latter likely being situated in the basement.

When Jay LaFlesch purchased the property, there were still sinks and a drainage system that would have been used by a meat butcher. A historic preservation expert and brick/stonemason noted that the pillars and some of the walls were still covered with a lime plaster that he said would have been consistent with sanitary procedures at the time.[49] Incidentally, there was no trace of the same material for the meat market that was in the Piece of Mind property.

Currently, the sidewalk void is open and flows into the main area of the basement. This was not always the case. According to the Sullivan sidewalk report, it had a wall with two doorways separating it from the rest of the basement.[50] The void was eight feet, four inches deep, and the current basement plan map illustrates the remnants of this wall. Above the smaller (two feet, two inches) doorway, there were stairs down into the void from the street, but these had already been removed by the 1981 report.

Archaeological Survey

During the survey, the basement was mapped and nineteen features recorded. The feature numbers are shown on the map. Of particular interest would be Feature 2, three ten- by twelve-inch beams supported by six ten- by ten-inch posts. These posts and beams of larch-wood composition provide primary structural support and are likely from the 1891 building.

Feature 4 is a doorway that was likely the original 1891 back door until an addition was added circa 1912. The current stairs and door are noted as Features 1 and 19. There are recessed cutouts in the doorframe for hinges that are no longer there. Feature 11 is a rectangular access in the ceiling to the upper floor. It appears there may have been stairs there at one time, and the 1902 Sanborn map does have stairs illustrated in that same location. Further evidence of the stairs might be found with Feature 12, a wooden frame that appears to be a doorway directly to the side of the opening above in the ceiling. The doorway is three feet, three inches wide, six feet, three inches high and three feet, three inches from the wall, suggesting a staircase along this east wall. Feature 15 is the stovepipe opening shared with Piece of Mind next door.

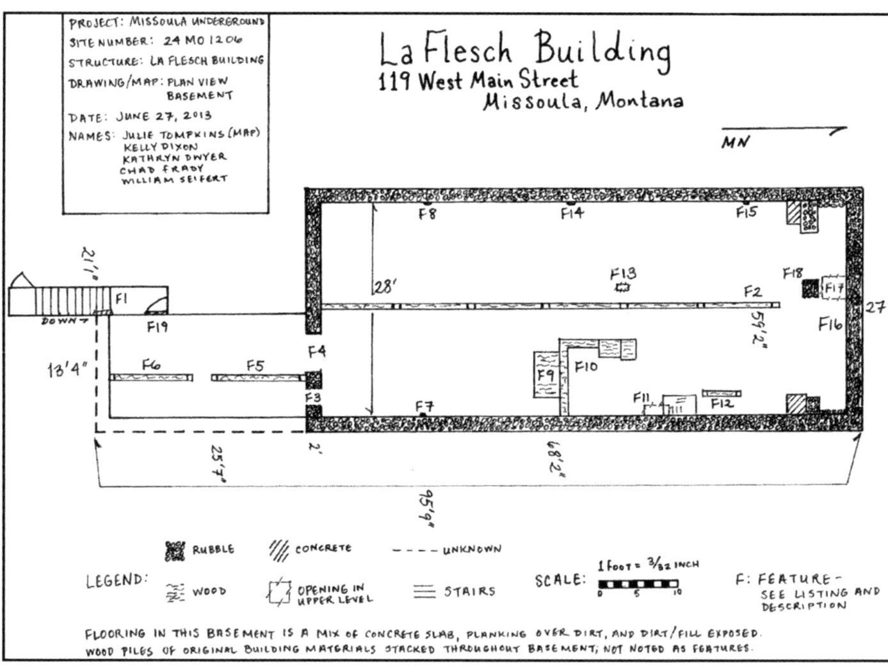

Plan map of the basement and sidewalk void for the LaFlesch building. *Map by Julie Tompkins.*

There is a also a three-foot-square steel door in the ceiling of the sidewalk void that was most likely put in after the stair access from the street was removed. Until recently, the remaining opening was used for delivery access.

As for steam pipes or tunnels, it is difficult to discern whether the steam pipe shown on the city steam tunnel map coming north from the alley behind the building was for the LaFlesch building. The city steam tunnel map is a rough drawing with no addresses or building delineations. Except for the larger, easily recognizable buildings that cover an entire block, such as the Hammond Building or the Missoula Mercantile, it is not possible to determine to which buildings the pipes are attaching. There is an opening coming through the far south wall that could have been for a steam pipe, but there is no pipe in place. The opening may also have been part of the building's drainage system and/or held a water pipe. Either way, this would have been only a pipe and not a tunnel access.

Summary Analysis

Built around the same time as most of the other properties in this study, circa 1891, the building here was erected for the *Missoula Gazette*, owned and operated by A.B. Hammond. A saloon, offices and lodgings operated above ground, and the basement contained the newspaper's water-powered printing system. Even after the building became part of the *Missoulian* complex, printing was still carried out in the basement.

After the newspaper vacated, the building housed a meat market and refrigeration plant in the basement. The building is not known to have ever been associated with a Chinese business, although a wooden structure that once served as a Chinese store at the same site/location was torn down to build the current property. While there may have been a steam pipe connected through the basement at one time, there is no steam tunnel access or any other tunnel access for that matter. The sidewalk void was fairly small and likely only used for deliveries and storage at one time before the wall was removed to connect the flow directly with the basement.

Riverside Café

The building located here at 247 West Front Street is a two-story brick commercial structure with a decorative cornice. There are two doors on

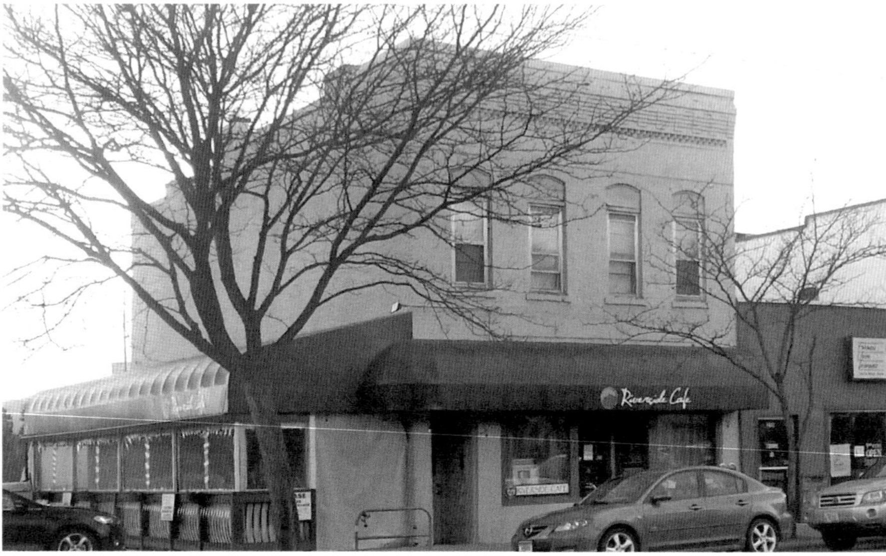

Riverside Café, formerly located at 245–247 West Front. *Author's collection.*

the north/street side of the building. The entry on the eastern side provides access to the first-floor business, and the door on the west side provides access to the second-floor apartments.

Historical Background

This property is located in what was colloquially known as Chinatown and the red-light district or "Tenderloin District" well into the 1920s.[51] The Sanborn maps for this part of town show quite a few buildings labeled as "Chinese," and the Plat Map for this portion of West Front Street from 1915 confirms a number of "cribs," also known as "female boarding," both terms for houses of prostitution.

Conducting historical research on most of these properties was challenging, but this particular property was probably the most difficult of them all. Keeping records for the area where the Chinese immigrants and prostitutes lived was not exactly high priority for the community. Moreover, fires were very common in that part of town. Most of the buildings were wood-frame structures that were easily and frequently destroyed. This makes it difficult to discern the dates for buildings or parts of buildings, such as basements/foundations.

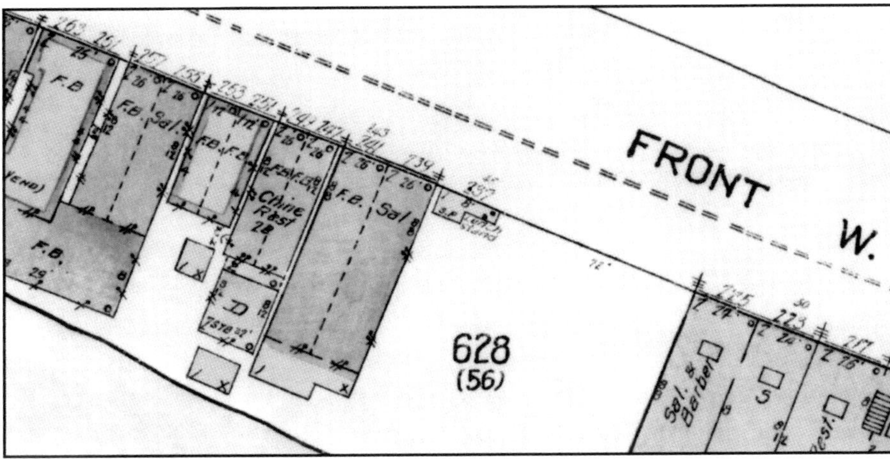

A detail of a 1912 Sanborn Fire Insurance Map showing the Chinese restaurant on the second floor. *Map used with permission from Environmental Data Resources Inc.*

Looking to the Sanborn maps, from 1884 to 1888, the buildings change a great deal, as does the landscape. In 1884, the majority of buildings in this section of the block are Chinese dwellings. There was a Chinese store in the location that could be the same land plot as the Riverside Café. By 1888, female boarding takes over in that area of Front Street. Street numbers other than 1, 2, 3 and so on are not used until 1893, and the numbers shift drastically as new buildings are erected in that area. In 1890, the Chinese store is still in the same location among all of the female boarding, but the building has changed enough to think that it is possibly a new building. After being a one-story building with a shingle roof, it became a two-story structure with a basement. In 1893, it seems to have finally succumbed to female boarding and was no longer labeled as Chinese. This was the same year that the famous madam Mary Gleim completed a new building only two doors to the west.

The next major change occurred between 1902 and 1912. While the footprint was similar, windows changed, and the building was split in two with an interior wood-frame wall. Another smaller structure to the rear of the building was labeled as a dwelling. It is unclear whether the dwelling was still connected to the main building. Both sides of the main building, on the first floor at least, were documented female boarding with a Chinese restaurant on the second floor. According to the Polk Directory for 1911, this is the Palace Café and Noodle Parlor, Mon Foo proprietor. The address for the restaurant is listed as 245 West Front Street. The Polk Directory also lists a business as Chinese Merchandise located at 247 West Front in the same building, yet this business does not appear on the Sanborn map, leading to the suggestion of the store being in the basement. The basement's storefront-like features observed during our fieldwork provide an additional line of evidence and will be discussed further in the archaeological survey section following.

In 1921, the building became two dwellings—one on either side of the split. According to the Missoula Fire Department scrapbook, the entire building was destroyed in 1930 due to an "unknown cause."[52] It is unknown how many buildings were destroyed at that time, but by 1957, there was no building on either side of 245–249 West Front Street. Even today, the Riverside Café is on the corner of the block with no building to its east.

Archaeological Survey

During the archaeological survey, the usual mapping and feature recording was conducted, but this particular basement raised a lot of questions due to the interesting architectural features found there. The building foundation/basement walls are brick, covered with white-painted wide plank boards. On both the east and west walls, there are built-in wood shelves with detailed molding, all painted white as well. The ceiling is white-painted bead board. This gives the basement a "finished" look, with a general storefront appearance.

The basement can currently be accessed in two ways. There is a modern addition to the south (rear) of the building that has a door into the basement. The other is an opening in the Riverside Café kitchen floor in about the same area where the original building connects to the modern addition. Inside the floor opening are steep stairs that resemble a ladder more than a staircase. There are also support poles in the center of the basement that are set in a north–south line, as if left over from when the building above was split in two circa 1912.

Unfortunately, this property was outside the priority area of the Sullivan sidewalk report, and it is unknown whether a secondary area inspection was ever conducted. Regardless, this property has a sealed (and possibly filled) sidewalk void beneath the north side (Front Street) of the building that is quite unique from others that have been viewed.

This basement is currently used for storage, as well as a small office for the Riverside Café. The priority features were two bay windows and a door (Features 1, 2 and 3) situated at the far north wall. Based on previous

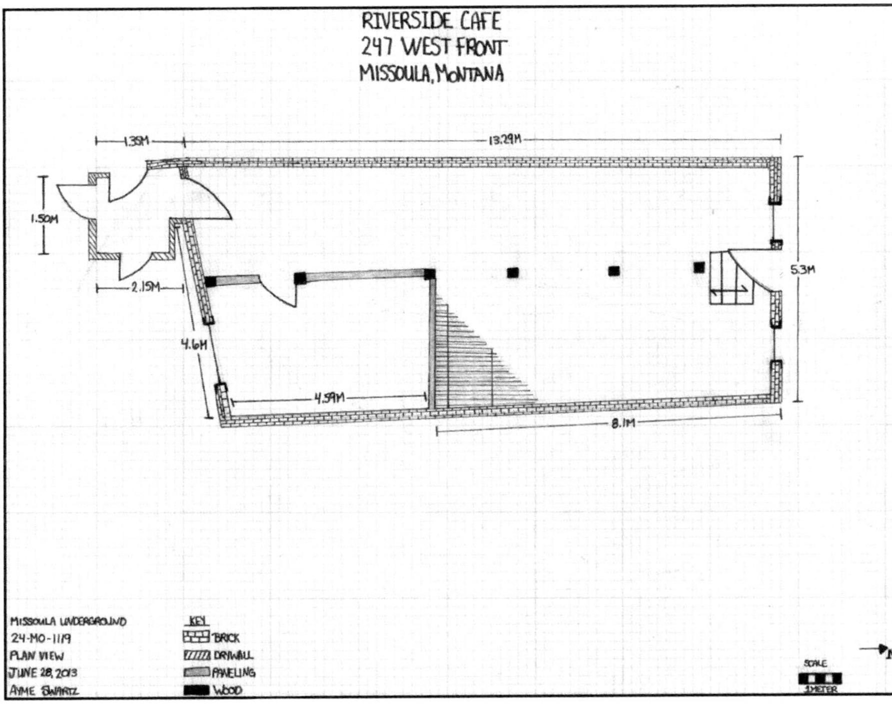

Plan map of the Riverside Café basement also depicting the large door entrance and windows (right) to the sealed sidewalk void. *Map by Ayme Swartz.*

experience with other underground features in Missoula, it is inferred that a sidewalk void once lay (or still exists) behind the other side of the door and windows. These features located at the building line would lead under the sidewalk. Feature 1 is a window on the west side of the north-facing wall. This is a recessed window with a decorative cast-iron handle for opening. Sections of the wood frame remain, but the glass is broken. The window is sealed with wide plank wood and concrete. The east window on the north wall was designated as Feature 3. This window is higher above the floor than the other and resembles a bay window shape, with some glass intact. Unlike Feature 1, this window has no discernible wood trim or handle but has been boarded up in the same way as Feature 1.

Feature 2 is a door between the two windows. The door is rather large, measuring one meter across and two meters in height. Inside the wood-frame door is a brick archway. The opening is, like the windows, sealed with wide wood planks on the inside and concrete on the other side. The wood planks and concrete likely provided the barrier when the void was filled.

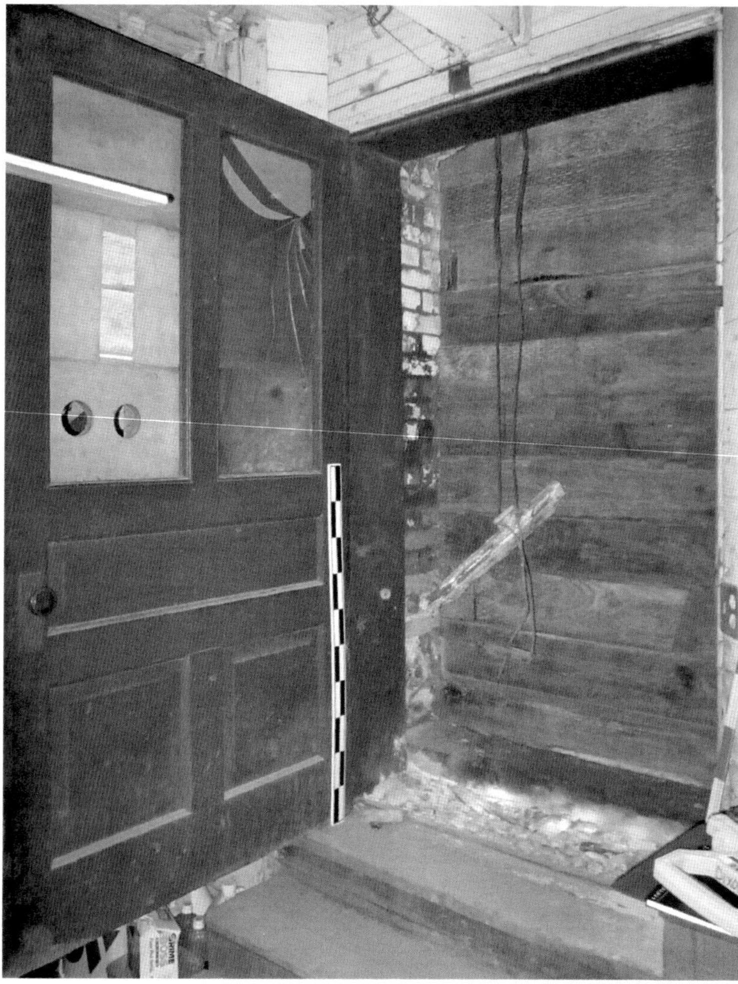

The door presumably leading to a sidewalk void in the basement of the Riverside Café. *Photo by Mary Bobbitt.*

The door itself is wooden with two windows in the top half (one of which is broken), a single decorative panel across the width of the door below those and two more decorative panels under that. The door also has a decorative brass doorknob. There are three steps leading up from the basement floor to this door. The most puzzling part of this feature is the door buzzer to the east of the door, inside the basement. Its location *inside* the door suggests that one had to take action to access something on the other side of the door within an underground feature, such as a sidewalk void.

On the east side of the interior south- and rear-facing wall is a pair of double-hung windows. These are also boarded up, likely because of the previously mentioned modern building on the other side. Because of the drastic slope to the river on which this building is situated, the south elevation wall is actually above ground, even though it is part of the basement. The south-facing windows would have looked toward—and been directly above—the river during the late nineteenth and early twentieth centuries. From the 1890 Sanborn map onward, there are windows shown on that south wall, further suggesting that this basement is original to the circa 1890 building when it became a more substantial and permanent two-story building with a basement.

Returning to the question of the Chinese store ("Chinese Merchandise" listed in the 1911 Polk Directory) as being located at 247 West Front Street yet not appearing on the 1912 Sanborn map with the female boarding (first floor) and Chinese restaurant (second floor), consider the results of the archaeological survey. The finished look of the basement, the windows facing the river, the rather elaborate windows and door into a sidewalk void and the built-in shelving could collectively present the appearance of a relatively well-finished store. In this context, the elaborate door and door buzzer might have served a functional purpose related to a store's daily operations or something else. Thus, the archaeological and architectural features in the basement strongly suggest that a store operated out of the basement during the early twentieth century. Whether it was definitely Chinese owned, however, is unknown.

Summary Analysis

To summarize, this property was once located in the heart of Chinatown and the red-light district. Buildings changed frequently in this area of town. Most were wood-frame structures that burned easily, and archival records are scant. Based on the Sanborn maps, the property was Chinese-occupied from at least 1884 to 1893, when it became all female boarding. During that time, the building footprint appears to change a few times. By 1912, the Sanborn map shows female boarding on the first floor and a Chinese restaurant on the second, whereas the Polk Directory entry notes a "Chinese Merchandise" establishment at this location. Experience with Sanborn maps during this project has shown that often whatever was located in the basement was not shown on the map, so it is possible the store was located in the basement.

The archaeological survey and the features recorded at this property reveal the presence of a store-like establishment in the basement based on the built-in shelving, the bead-board ceiling and the wood-paneled wall covering the brick structural wall. The grand entrance and the windows next to it also suggest a fairly upscale establishment. Data from other properties might suggest this doorway was a sidewalk entrance to the store, but unfortunately, without any knowledge of the sidewalk void, it is not possible at this time to make a definitive claim that a sidewalk void even exists. It may have been possible that the basement establishment merely connected this way to the female boarding or restaurant above it. Although it would be pure speculation, a discreet access point to the female boarding above could explain the doorbell inside the basement at the doorway. Access to the basement would have been possible on the south (rear) side of the building close to the river as a way to not be seen entering the female establishment upstairs.

Missoula Mercantile and Garden City Drug

The final property is the Missoula Mercantile, referred to by the community as the "Merc." The Merc was the center of commerce and society in Missoula from approximately 1877 to 1955. The original part of the building that represents the southwest corner of the current property was erected in 1877. There were multiple additions over the years that expanded the Merc's square footage, so it became the large, rectangular two-and-one-

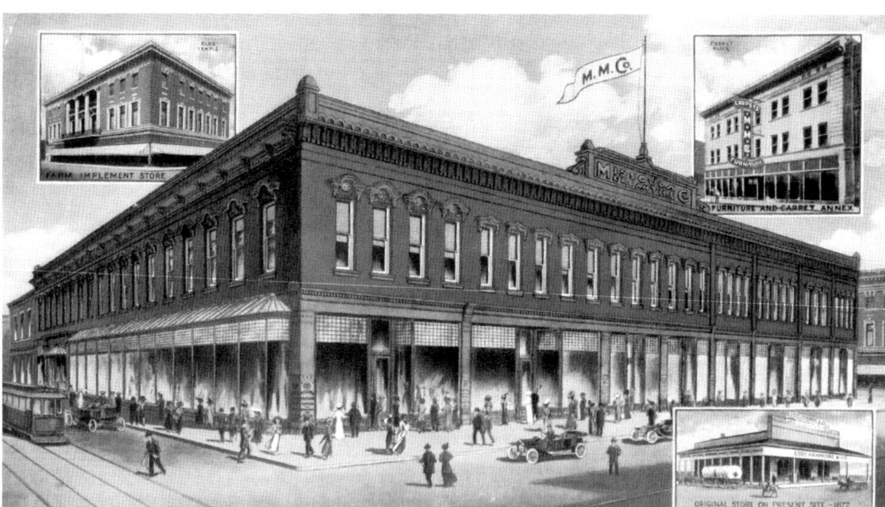

An artist's illustration of the Missoula Mercantile at the corner of Higgins Avenue and East Front Street. *Photo No. 78.12.170, Archives and Special Collections, Mansfield Library, University of Montana.*

half-story building that it is today. After the Merc went out of business, the building continued to serve as an anchor-store location. It became the Bon Marche department store in 1959, the Bon-Macy's in 1999 and Macy's in 2005. The building has been vacant since Macy's closed in 2010, but a new owner, Octagon Partners, purchased the building in 2011 and began the process of restoring the Mercantile to its former historic glory.

Historical Background

The Missoula Mercantile began as a small log structure on West Front Street, then known as Bonner and Welch before it became E.L. Bonner and Company (1871) and Eddy Hammond and Company (1876). In 1877, A.B. Hammond contracted to build the new structure at the current location, but it did not officially become the Missoula Mercantile Company until 1885.[53] This property is slightly different from the others in the sense that it did not change as far as what types of businesses occupied the space, but the Sanborn maps show how the building changed over the years with additions, renovations and movement of departments from one area of the store to another. A.B. Hammond was a shrewd businessman who managed to contract with the Northern Pacific Railroad to supply the timber needed for building the railroad, as well as all other necessary supplies that he could supply from his Mercantile. As the company rapidly grew, it also became the largest employer in Missoula. Whatever a person

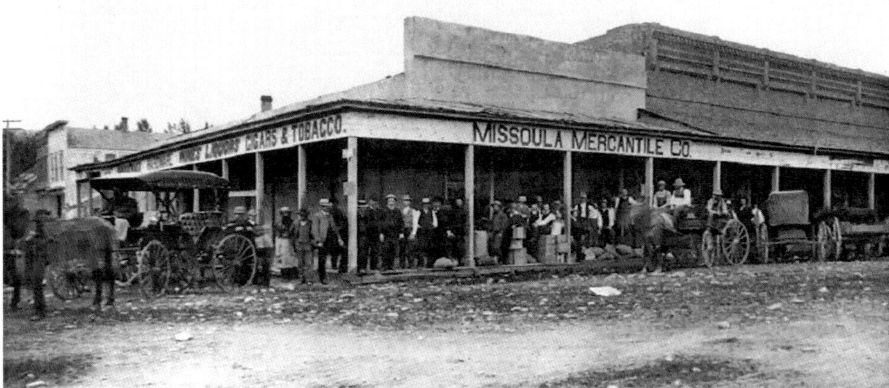

Missoula Mercantile, circa 1885. *Photo No. 70.0113, Archives and Special Collections, Mansfield Library, University of Montana.*

could possibly need, the Merc had or could get. It was the largest retail store and wholesale supplier between Fort Benton in eastern Montana and Walla Walla, Washington.

The Merc building was almost demolished in 1946. Records show that in that year, the company was considering a renovation, but the architectural firm from Chicago, Markham Ashberry, actually suggested that the entire building be demolished and rebuilt. Walter McLeod, the president and manager at the time, considered this as a possibility but decided it would be prudent to wait until more information was received about post–World War II taxation. Neither the demolition of the building nor the renovations suggested by the firm from Chicago ever occurred.

One of the biggest reasons the Merc was considered inherent to this project, other than it being the heart of the city, is that oral history interviews revealed the existence of tunnels, possibly separate from the steam tunnels, that were used for other reasons than steam tunnel access. There is reportedly a tunnel running east–west under Higgins Avenue connecting the Merc with the Florence Hotel across the street to the west that was used by John Wayne, the famous western movie actor. While the tunnel is gone, the door still exists in the west wall of the original Merc basement.[54] This

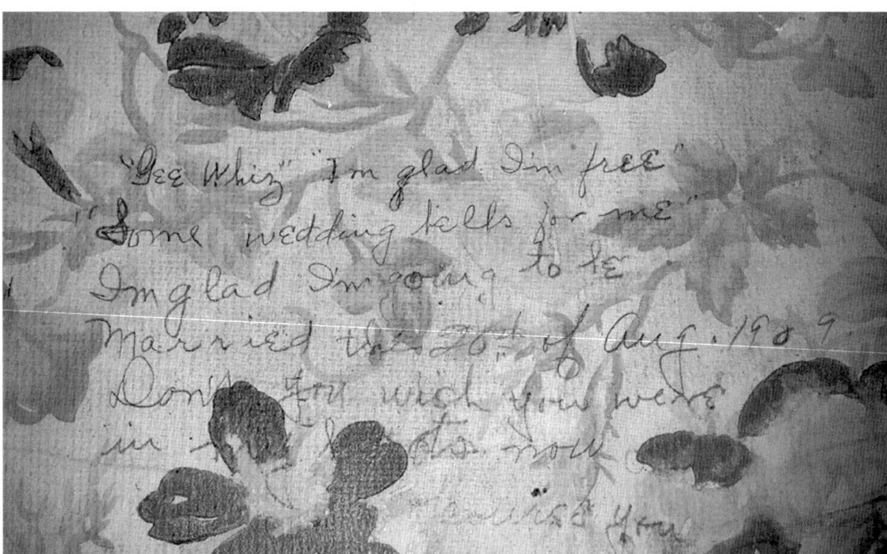

Graffiti on the wall of the second floor of the Missoula Mercantile. The Mercantile was a popular place for the latest fashions in wedding apparel. *Author's collection.*

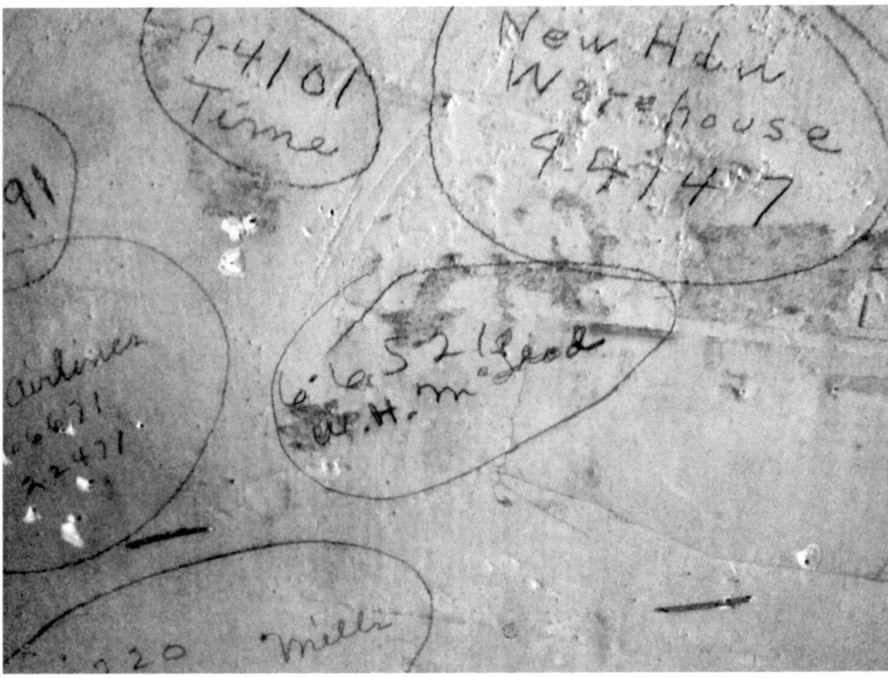

The Mercantile was a bustling business with a wide network, as shown by the phone extensions written on the wall near what was once the loading dock. *Author's collection.*

will be discussed further in the survey section. There was also another tunnel connecting from the Merc's southern sidewalk void to the First National Bank across East Front Street. At one time, the Merc actually supplied the money used by the bank instead of the other way around. The money (cash) was kept safe in a bank-like vault near the Merc offices in the center of the building. The tunnel would have allowed for safer passage between the two. This is a separate feature from the sidewalk void (described further below) that is now sealed and inaccessible.

The Missoula Mercantile at one time had rather extensive sidewalk voids on both the south and west sides of the building. On the west side, a long void ran the length of the building; Garden City Drug, also on the west (northwest) side of the building, had two smaller voids adjacent to the Merc's long sidewalk void. The void along the south side of the Merc did not run along the entire block but was also quite long at 109 feet, 1 inch according to the Sullivan sidewalk report drawing. The three voids along the west side were filled prior to the 1981 study, but the south-side void was still intact. All but the far northern section of the void on the east side have been sealed and/or filled. Prior to that there were five entrances from the basement to the void and four brick arches within the void connecting those entrances and providing structural support.

Archaeological Survey

The archaeological survey for this building produced three maps: Area 1) the southwest section of the Merc basement; Area 2) the basement of Garden City Drug; and Area 3) a perplexing system of tunnels internal to the basement. Features in all of these areas were recorded, and crews recovered artifacts from Areas 2 and 3. The double name and site number should be noted. The northwest corner of the building was at one time the Garden City Drug store. It is technically a separate brick structure built between 1893 and 1902 that became incorporated into the Merc complex around 1934. The building does have a separate listing on the National Register and thus a site number different from the Merc. Part of the basement in which research was conducted was the basement of the drugstore before it became the liquor and tobacco department for the Merc. It is also important to note that only the oldest portion (southwest corner) of the Mercantile building was surveyed due to the immense size of the entire basement.

The Garden City Drug basement is the subject of the Area 2 plan map for its fascinating features and because this was the room in which surface collection of artifacts occurred. During the original reconnaissance trip, this basement space had already been deconstructed down to the bare bones for renovation. The walls were composed of the stone masonry that has become typical of the basements examined. The plank floor had to be removed because the wood was no longer salvageable.[55] This removal of the wood left behind the original dirt floor, which contained artifacts scattered about the space that were recovered.

During the first day of work on site, an entrance to a crawl space was discovered in a small room with metal-clad flooring in Area 1. After brief exploration, it was determined that the crawl space was rather extensive and included tunnel-like excavations in the dirt foundation below the southwest (and oldest) part of the Merc. The tunnels resemble mine construction and look like hand-dug channels. Part of this area is under the original Merc structure, and another part is under the first addition. This space became part of the study and was mapped as Area 3.

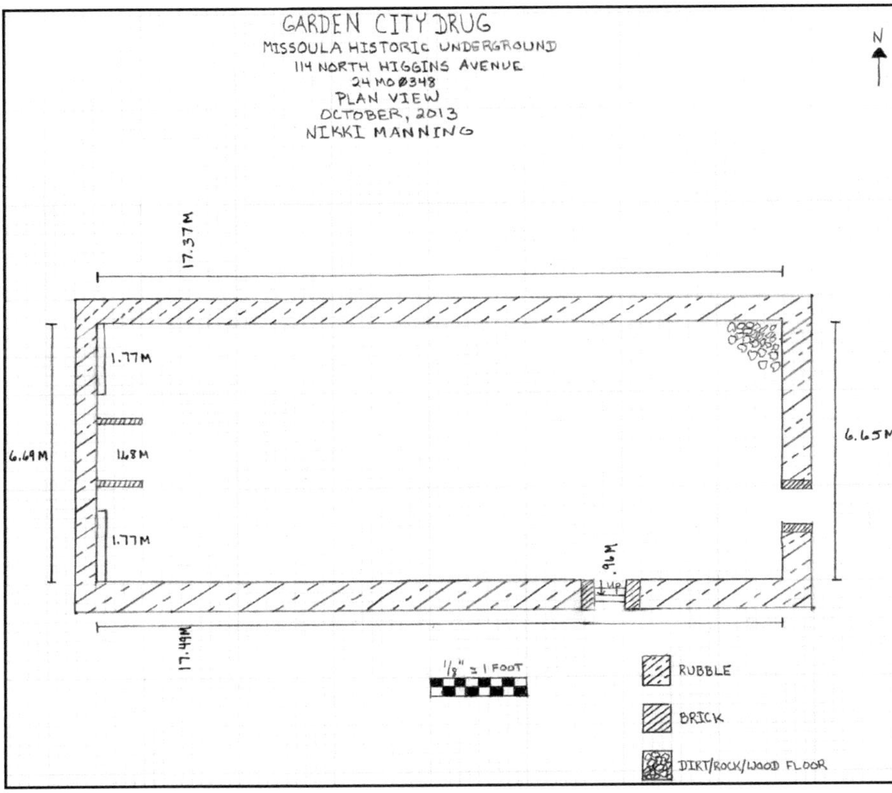

Plan map of Area 2 in the basement of the Missoula Mercantile. *Map by Nikki Manning.*

Archaeologists, architects, historical architects, preservationists, historic masons and oral history informants have been flummoxed by the features after observing this basement space. The features (the dirt walls, the beams providing structural support, the rails in the tunnel floor that appear to have been used for moving a cart and the brackets that once held pipes) all suggest that the small tunnels were definitely dug out of the foundation after that part of the building was erected. It is quite possible that it was dug out for the purpose of running pipes. There is wood-beam construction that supports the floor above, so it is possible the tunnels were dug to place these reinforcements. One historic preservationist and mason noted the dimples in the wood next to most of the nails. He suggested that the work had possibly been performed with poor lighting or by unskilled apprentices, even children.[56] There are also several modern concrete supports. When two other historic masons

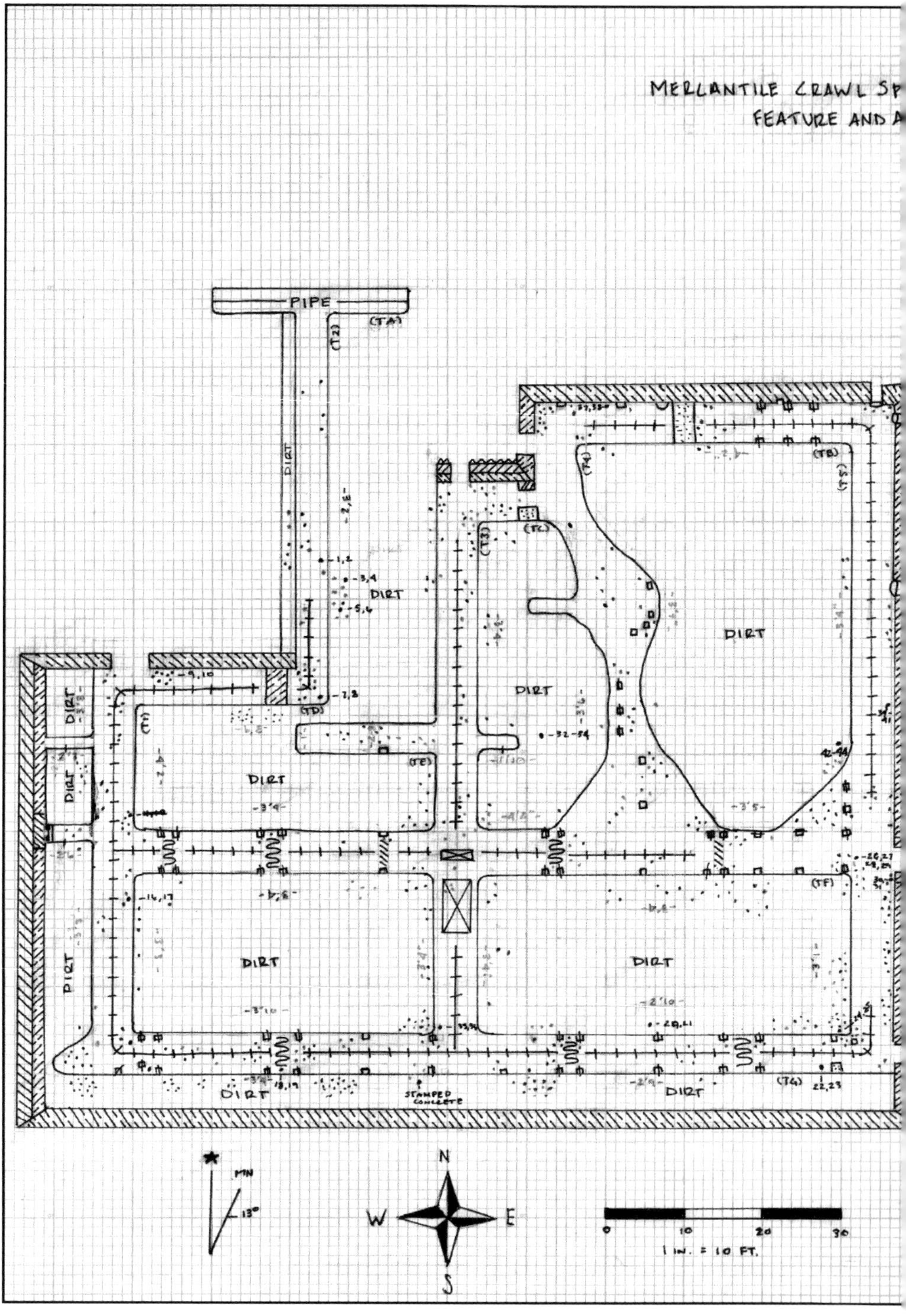
MERCANTILE CRAWL SP
FEATURE AND A
PIPE
DIRT
STAMPED CONCRETE
MN
13°
N
S
W
E
0
10
20
30
1 IN. = 10 FT.

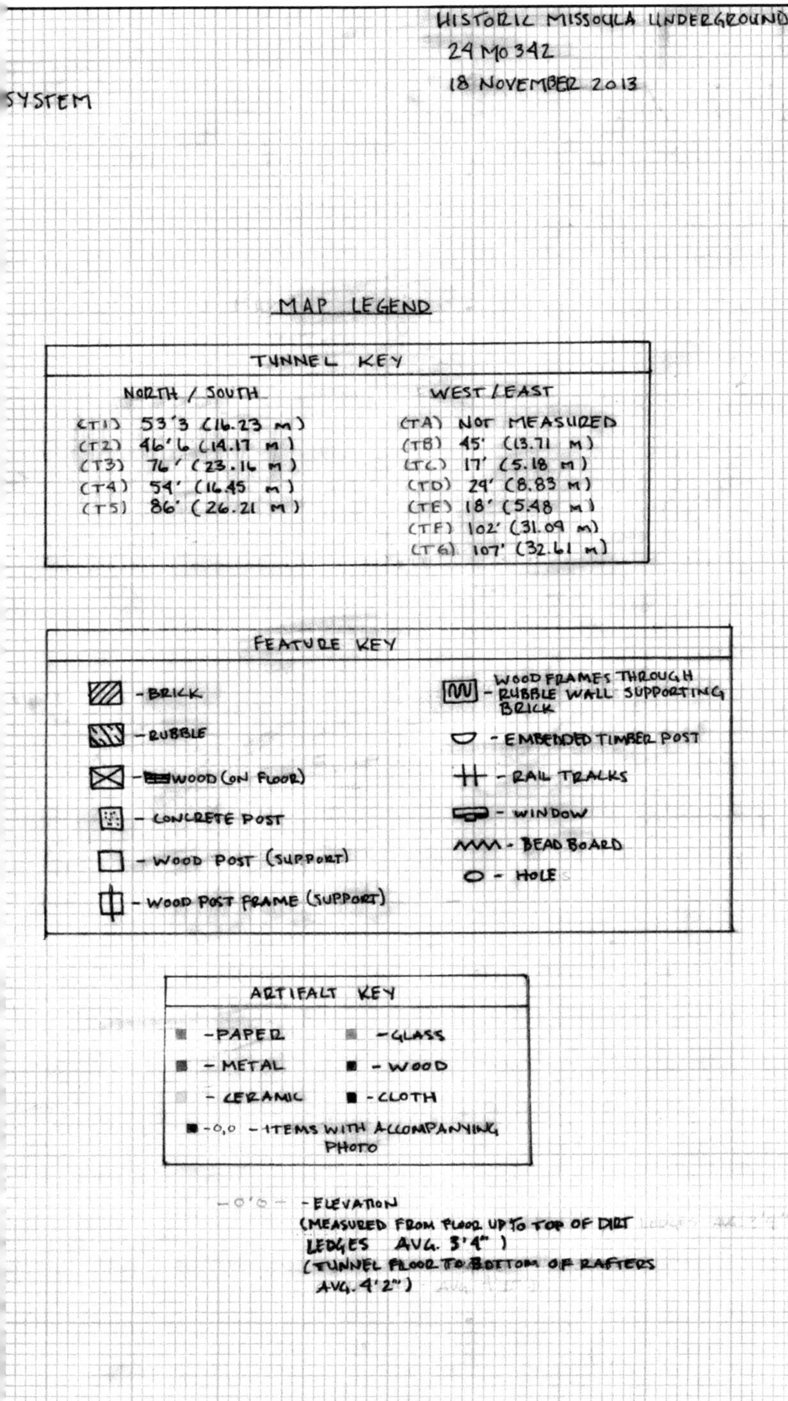

Plan map of Area 3 in the basement of the Missoula Mercantile. *Map by Kelli Casias.*

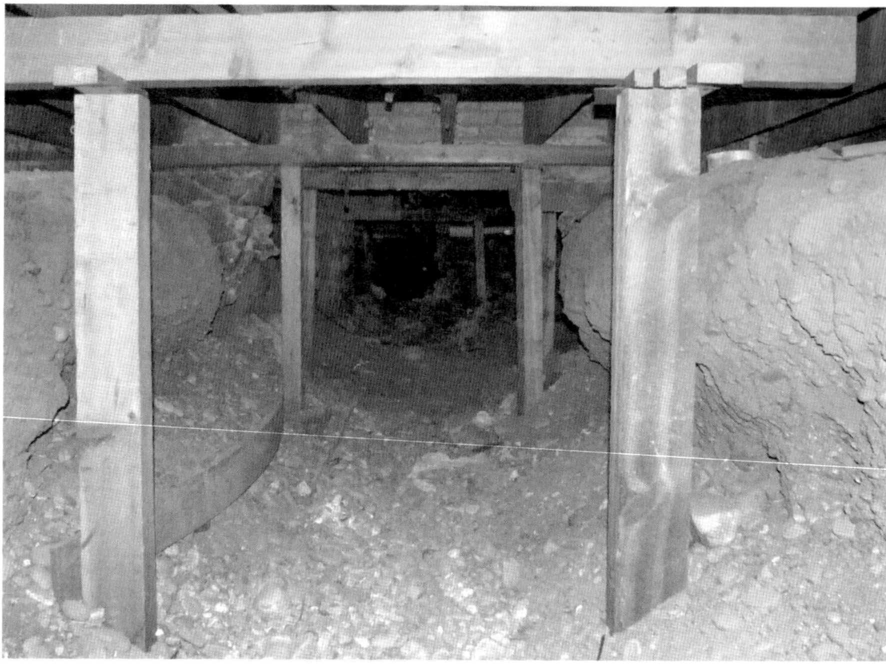

Above: Crawl space timber-beam supports in the Missoula Mercantile basement tunnels resemble construction often found in mines. *Photo by Kelli Casias.*

Opposite, top: Archaeology student Dylan Kemp (six feet tall) demonstrates the scale of the crawl space tunnels in the Missoula Mercantile basement. The concrete supports can be seen in this image as well. *Photo by Kelli Casias.*

Opposite, bottom: The reported "John Wayne tunnel" door. Inside the double wooden swinging doors is a blocked off archway that once led to the sidewalk void and possibly a tunnel under Higgins Avenue. *Author's collection.*

toured through the space, they dated the area as possibly post-1945, which just deepens the mystery.[57]

Features were recorded in all three areas, the only difference being that in Area 3, due to the constraining space, features were recorded directly onto the map as opposed to being fully recorded separately, as was the usual protocol. Twenty-six features were recorded in Areas 1 and 2. Many of the features are related to internal doorways, structural support for the building and pipes or openings that once held pipes. The features of most interest to this project, however, are the doors and windows leading underground.

One of these doorways is the rumored "John Wayne" door (Feature 16). This door is situated in the west wall of Area 1. There are two white, wooden

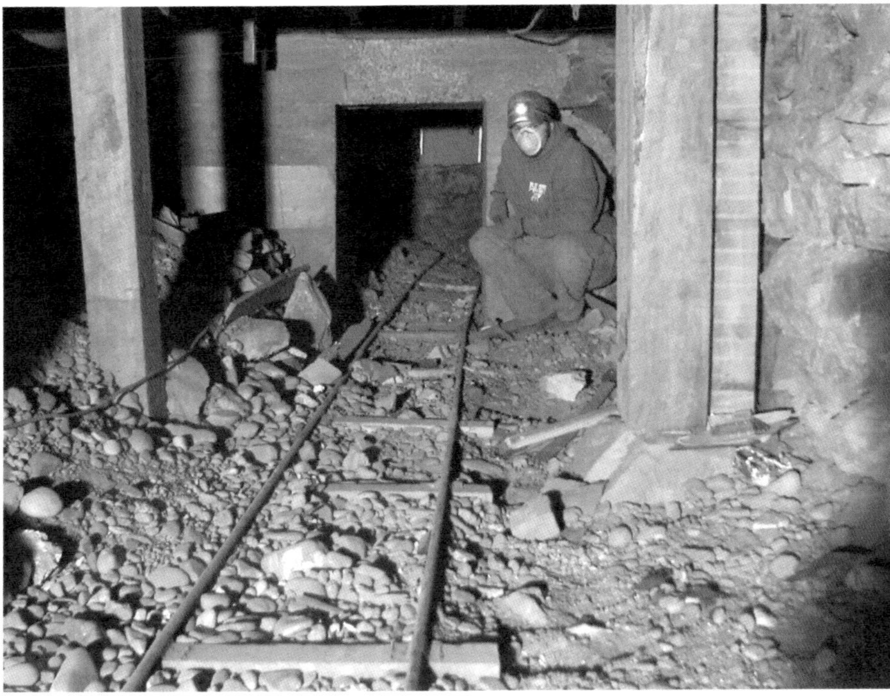

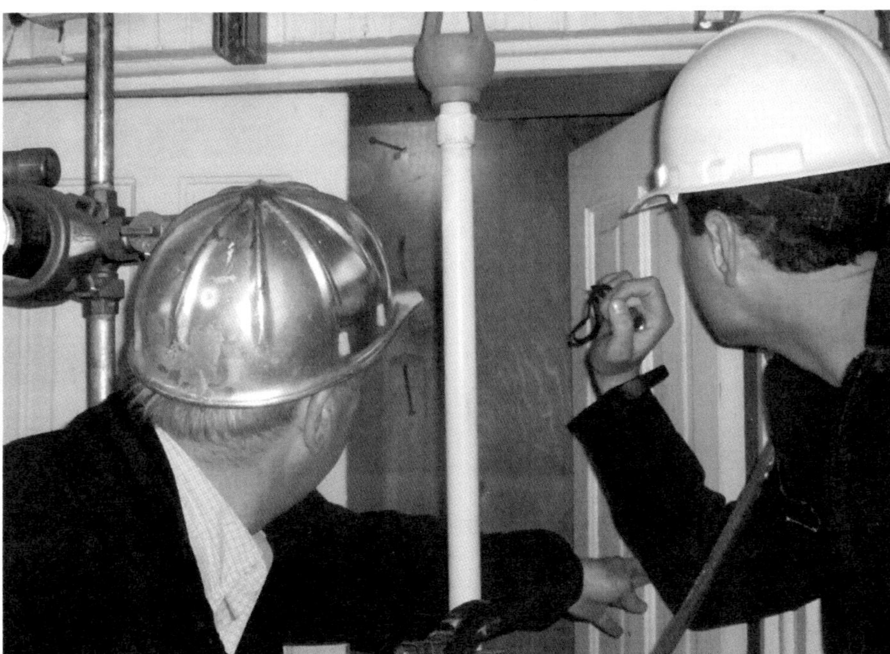

swinging doors attached to the opening, and behind them is an opening that is now sealed with concrete blocks. If one were still able to go through these doors, it is said this would lead directly to the tunnel providing access across the street to the Florence building. Since the void is sealed and filled, it is not possible at this time to confirm whether this is the iconic "John Wayne tunnel" entrance.

The other most interesting features are located in Area 2. Along the same west-facing wall as the "John Wayne" door is another extremely large door, with two very sizable windows to either side of it. These would have led into the two small sidewalk voids on the northwest part of the building, facing Higgins Avenue. According to the Sullivan Report, other than knowing there were once sidewalk voids there that were filled, it is unclear whether there may have once been stairs from the sidewalk that led down to this basement room.[58] If not stairs, there may have been the previously mentioned glass blocks in the sidewalk to provide light for the void space.

Artifact Recovery

During an earlier reconnaissance trip into the basement of the Mercantile before the fall project began, a tobacco pipe was found lying on the surface in Area 2. At this point, it was decided that maybe a surface collection was in order. This resulted in the collection of a large number of artifacts. There are a great number of glass shards, bottle parts, corks, metal pieces and paper among some more interesting items.

Artifacts were also recovered from Area 3. There were fewer items pulled from this area, but they are nonetheless quite intriguing, especially considering the unknown use of the crawl space tunnels. For some small items, the smallest being a bead from a piece of jewelry, it is easily understood that they could have fallen between the floorboards above. The larger items, however—a pair of men's dress shoes, for instance, or an old box with shipping label and postage still intact in which baby shoes were shipped from Danvers, Massachusetts, to the Missoula Mercantile—are more perplexing. A stack of pinned-together receipts from 1888 was found, as well as sardine cans, bottles, candy wrappers, advertising booklets and comic books. The things that could not have fallen through the cracks from above suggest that people were using this crawl space rather frequently, and it was not just whoever dug the channels or maintenance workers. Not a single artifact recovered in these tunnels was of Chinese origin or even suggested Chinese use.

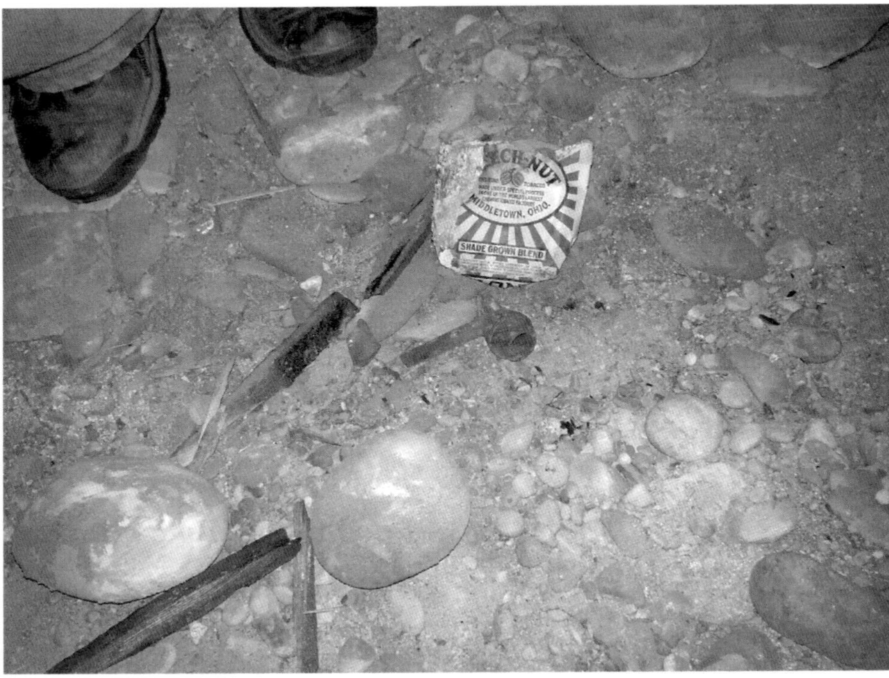

Wooden tobacco pipe with amber mouthpiece found on the floor in Area 2 of the Missoula Mercantile. Tobacco bag was found nearby and moved for scale and reference. *Author's collection.*

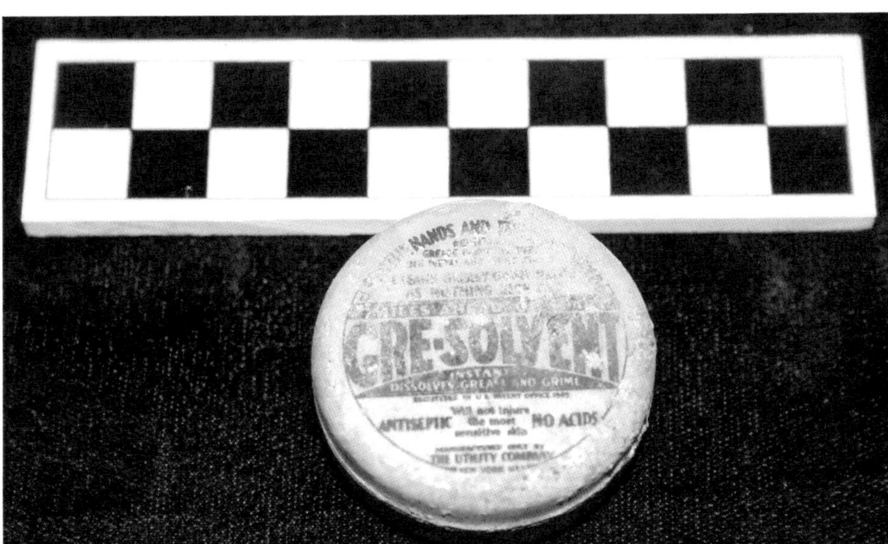

Tin of Gre-Solvent hand cleaner recovered during Area 2 surface collection. *Photo by Rachel Summers-Wilson.*

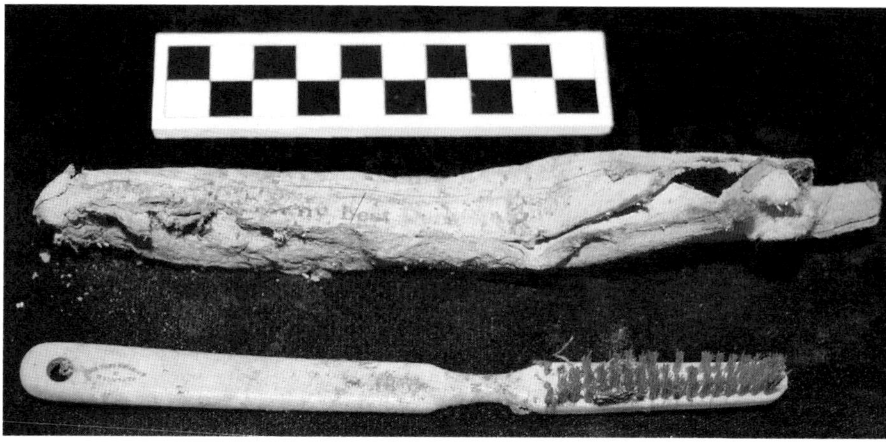

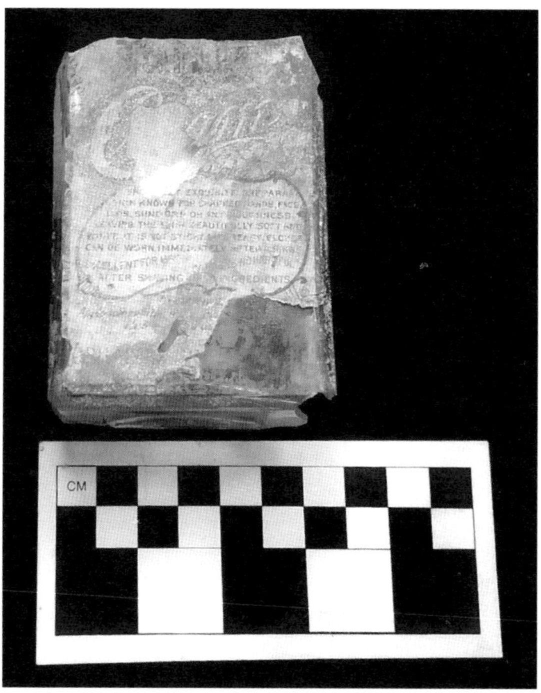

Above: Unused toothbrush and box recovered during Area 2 surface collection. *Photo by Rachel Summers-Wilson.*

Left: "Glam" men's aftershave/tonic square bottle recovered during Area 2 surface collection. The top and back of the bottle are broken. *Author's collection.*

Summary Analysis

This property was erected as the Missoula Mercantile and continued to be the Missoula Mercantile until approximately 1959. Commissioned by A.B. Hammond, the wealthiest businessman in Missoula, it is an impressive structure. This building certainly has (or did at one time) have access to the

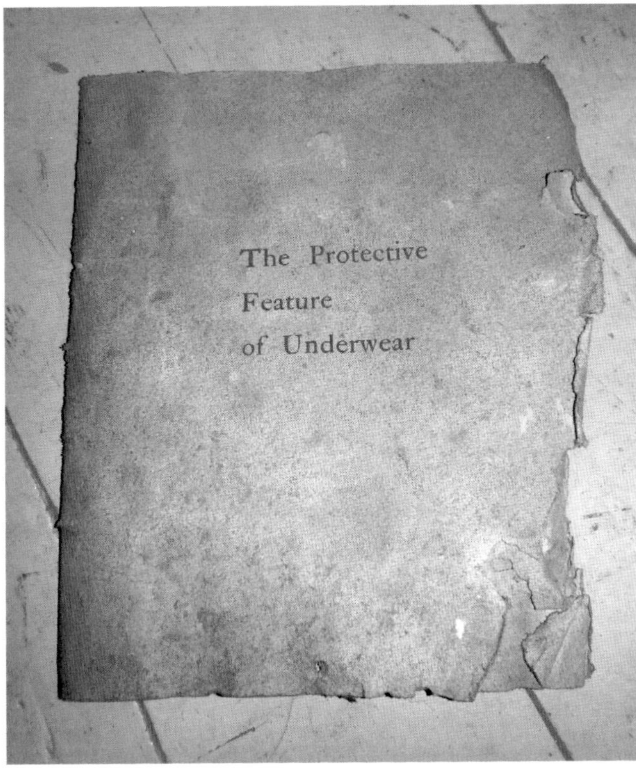

Right: "The Protective Feature of Underwear," written by a physician, primarily geared toward men and presumably an advertisement for undergarments, was recovered during Area 3 surface collection. *Author's collection.*

Below: A piece of stationery from the 1880s, when the Mercantile was still known as Eddy, Hammond & Co., recovered during Area 3 surface collection. *Author's collection.*

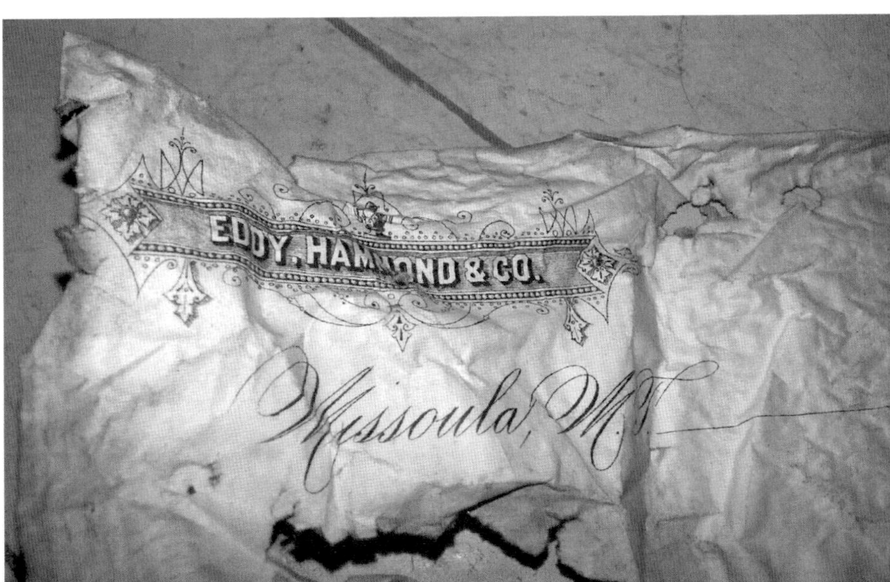

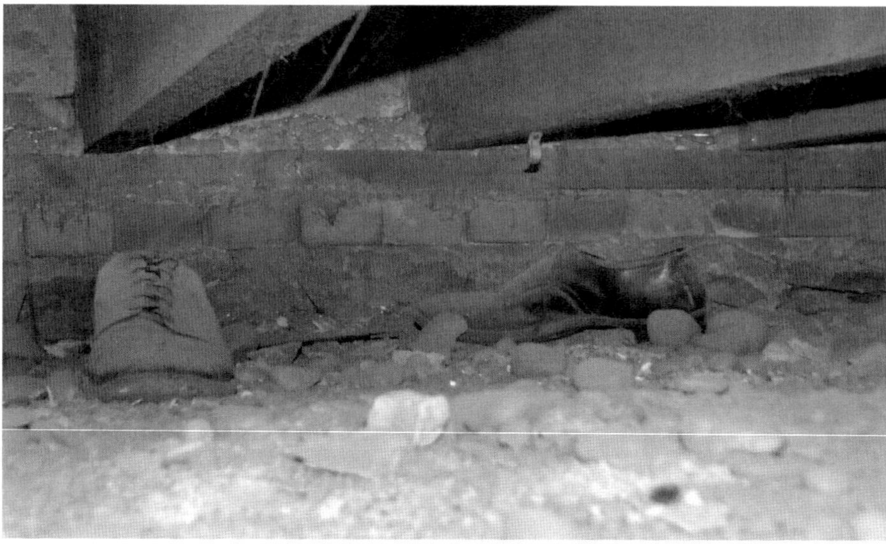

Men's dress shoes discovered on a ledge created by the dug-out tunnels in Area 3, found tucked approximately five feet back from the edge. The shoes are circa 2000, when the building was occupied by Macy's Department Store. *Photo by Kelli Casias.*

steam tunnels. A.B. Hammond and Walter McLeod, his right-hand man, were responsible for building the local steam plant near the river that made it necessary for steam pipes to be laid in a tunnel under Higgins Avenue in 1908.[59] A.B. Hammond supplied steam heat first to his buildings at the intersection of Higgins Avenue and Front Street (the Mercantile, the First National Bank, the Hammond Building and the Florence Hotel) and then added businesses that requested connection after that.

This immediately throws into question the "Chinese tunnels" under Missoula city streets. It is possible that Chinese labor was used to build the tunnels, thus leading to the "Chinese tunnel" myth, but there are two reasons to believe this was not the case. First, by 1908, the Chinese population in Missoula had diminished to approximately seventy-three individuals in all of Missoula County, according to the 1910 United States Census.[60] Second, it is unlikely A.B. Hammond would have hired Chinese labor. During a very public political fight in 1891 in which Hammond sought to discredit the mayoral candidate Frank Higgins, he printed in the *Missoula Gazette* that Higgins "was unsuitable [for the office of mayor] because he was unprogressive and because he employed Chinese."[61] While some of the recorded features for the Mercantile are connected to an underground, there is no evidence to connect any of these with the Chinese community, and there is actually documentary evidence to the contrary.

3

THE "CHINESE UNDERGROUND"

CHINESE IMMIGRANTS IN THE AMERICAN WEST

The Chinese Must Go!
—Workingmen's Party of California

For any analysis of past events, a historical context is essential, and in this case, the Chinese immigrant experience in the American West from 1870 to 1920 presents that contextual point of departure. Since our primary focus deals with a Chinese connection to the Missoula historic underground, this historical overview will also cover what information currently exists regarding so-called Chinese undergrounds and tunnels across the West. In a broader context, this is also part of the story of urbanization in the American West.

When Chinese immigrants began arriving in larger numbers to the United States during the California gold rush, they were already facing an uphill battle. It can be said that their so-called "reputation" preceded them. Chinese curiosities were already being displayed in some U.S. cities as "exotic yet dangerous."[62] These characteristics of exotic and dangerous applied to the immigrants as well as to their goods, creating a prejudiced and discriminatory environment. In 1880, thirty years after the immigration explosion (Chinese as well as European) that began in 1849, the United States and China signed a treaty giving the United States the right to limit Chinese immigration. The Chinese Exclusion Act was signed into law on March 6, 1882, prohibiting the entry of Chinese laborers for a period of ten years. Merchants and professionals were the only exception to this legislation. Ten years later, the Geary Act extended the exclusion and also required Chinese immigrants to register with local authorities. The Exclusion Act was renewed for another ten years in 1902, but in 1904, it was made indefinite and was not repealed until 1943, after the attack on Pearl Harbor in 1941 brought the United States and China into an alliance.[63]

During the California gold rush, most Chinese immigrants were placer miners. Since legislation existed that prevented nonwhites from staking claims for gold mining, groups of Chinese immigrants followed mining camps along rivers; once a camp picked up and left to explore new ore bodies, Chinese laborers mined what was left behind. When even this stopped being profitable, many turned to wage labor, which often involved working for mining companies and railroad construction. Ronald Takaki estimates that 90 percent of the railroad workforce consisted of Chinese immigrants.[64] When the gold rush boom was ending and the railroad was near completion in the late 1870s, people were moving en masse to urban centers, searching for work and different opportunities that only cities could provide. Chinese-owned businesses became more common, particularly laundries, which did not necessitate a large investment. The Chinese also became tenant farmers, agricultural workers, seafood harvesters and processors and domestic servants.[65]

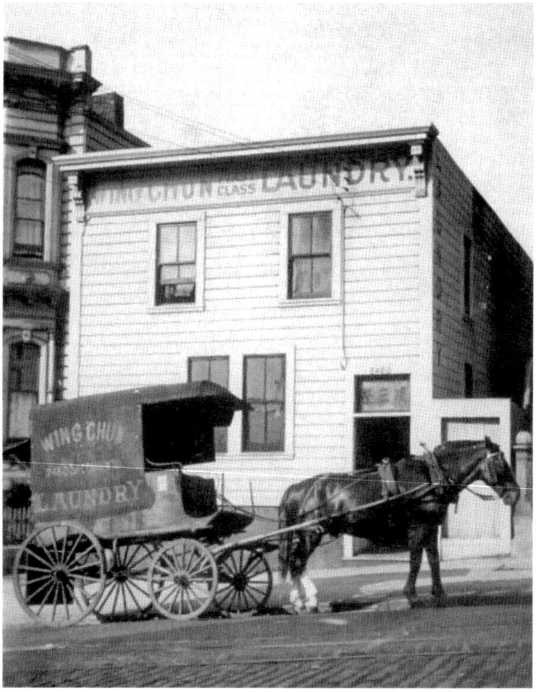

Chinese laundry wagon, Sacramento Street, 1906. *L. Slevin Collection, Photo #670, Bancroft Library, University of California–Berkeley.*

Unfortunately, the more the Chinese entered the wage-earning workforce and owned and operated businesses, the less they were tolerated, particularly by organized labor groups. The increase in the labor force made laborer jobs more difficult to find. The

Right, top: Illustration depicting that the Chinese were the only immigrant group "barred out." *Photo from Frank Leslie's Illustrated Newspaper.*

Right, bottom: "Chinese? No! No! No!" anti-Chinese rally advertisement from 1892. *Photo No. 1903.1.200, Washington State Historical Society.*

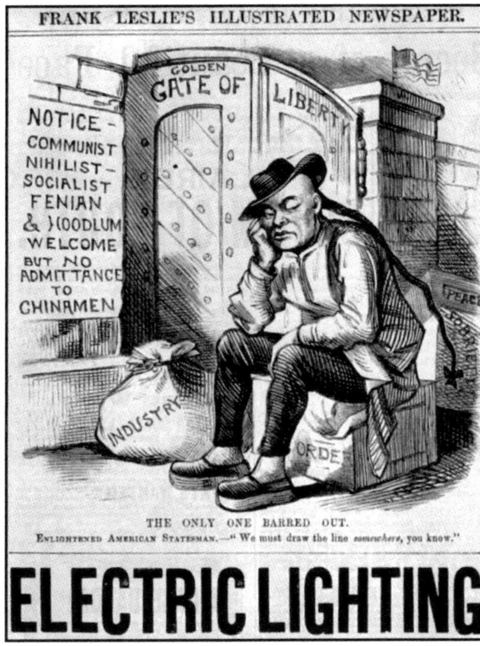

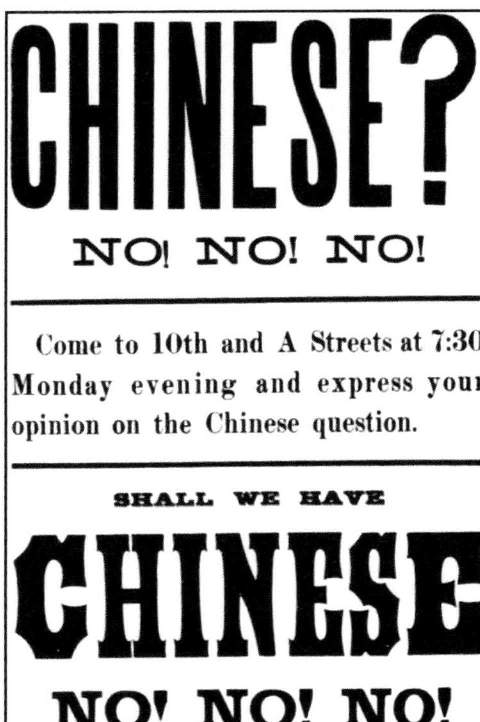

Chinese were always willing to accept lower wages for the same amount of work, and basically any savvy business owner is going to use that as a chance to increase revenue.[66] When European Americans were able to find a job, the wages had been driven down and they needed someone to blame for the current economic situation. The Chinese were easily differentiated and singled out.[67] One of the most outspoken of these labor groups was the Workingmen's Party of California. It was the creator of the well-known "the Chinese Must Go" campaign. At the height of its influence in 1877, a wave of violence swept throughout the American West.[68] Anti-Chinese sentiment turned from prejudice and discrimination to racist hatred and all-out war on Chinese immigrants, often instigated and sanctioned by government and local authorities.

The campaign against the Chinese was not only political

and economic, according to historian K. Scott Wong, but it was also cultural, affecting the Chinese immigrant community then and now.[69] Character assassination began well before the Chinese population started to grow in America. Because most of the first immigrants came during the gold rush and were male, they were either young bachelors or left their families behind in China. Legislation was enacted soon after, preventing further immigration and preventing families from joining them. It was actually believed by those with an anti-Chinese sentiment that the majority of Chinese women residing in the United States were actually prostitutes.[70] Gambling, as well as opium smoking practices, was often greatly sensationalized. More to the truth, the same people would often frequent the same location, generally a social club, and there would be free meals and gambling. It was not until these same places started attracting non-Chinese clientele that the public started paying attention. When police raids became frequent, these clubs and businesses were forced into hiding and secrecy, making them more nefarious than they actually were.[71] The historian Laverne Dicker's research provides evidence that there were opium dens in Chinatown, but most of the Chinese population could actually not afford the habit themselves.[72]

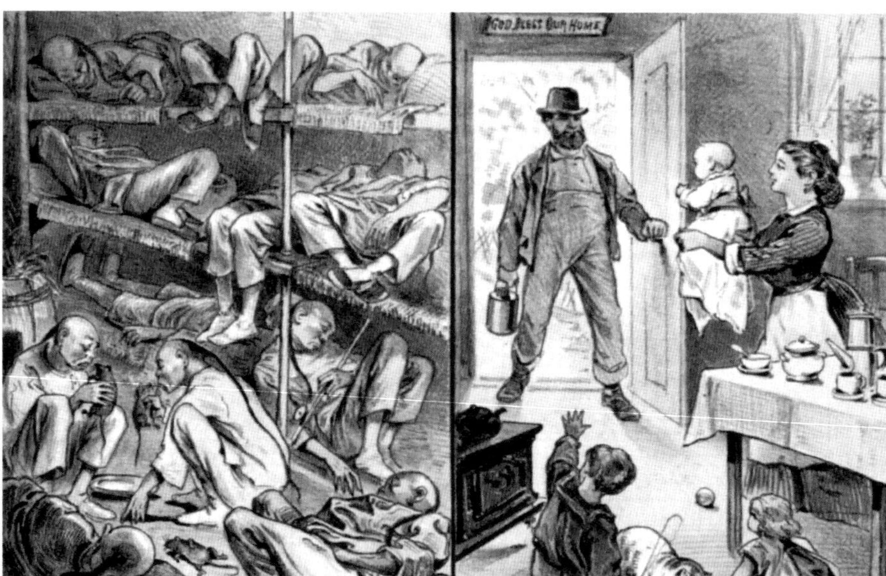

Caricature showing Chinese men, living in a very crowded opium den, eating rats; and an American man arriving home from work to his wife, children and "normal" household. The picture is meant to spark outrage, showing why the Chinese can live on such a low wage while others cannot. *Library of Congress, LC-USZC2-1242.*

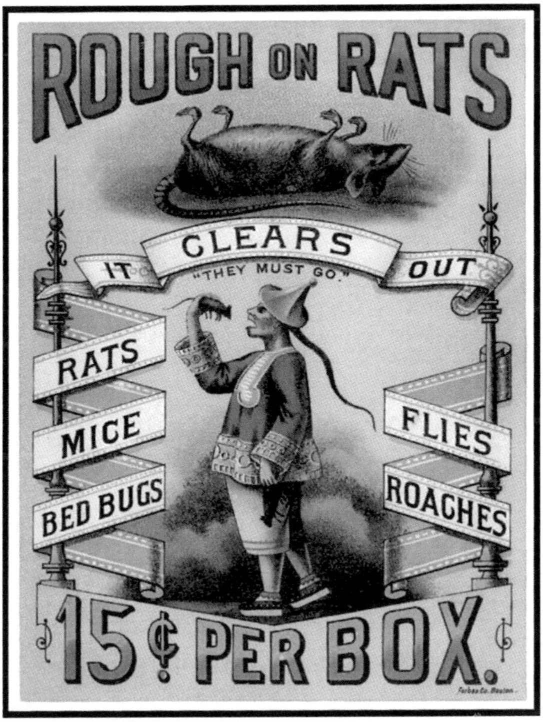

Anti-Chinese rat poison advertisement. *Viintage.com.*

The Chinese immigrants were often characterized as having a passive reaction to being harassed and discriminated against. Political cartoons showed Chinese fearfully fleeing the harassment, and businesses touted products at the expense of Chinese immigrants. For example, an advertisement for the new Missouri steam washing machine showed a washing machine with arms and legs chasing a Chinese laundry worker out of San Francisco all the way back to China. Another suggestive advertisement depicted a Chinese man eating a rat. The ad was for a rat poison company with the slogan "They Must Go!"—rats as well as the Chinese.[73]

In contrast, other scholars have noted that the Chinese were not always so passive. In some cases, they attempted to fight anti-Chinese legislation legally and in other ways.[74] The Woolen Mills Chinatown in San Jose, California, is a good example of the Chinese fighting back with ingenuity and expertise. In the 1880s, local ordinances were passed that required all new residences to be tied into the new city sewer system. Because the Woolen Mills Chinatown had recently been burned (arson), it required new residences and buildings. Thinking it would be too expensive for residents of Chinatown, non-Chinese citizens assumed this would be a way to get rid of the Chinatown scourge. To the contrary, archaeological excavation and historical research showed quite an extensive sewage system made of wood and ceramic, built by the Chinatown population to drain into the main sewage system for the city, making them fully compliant with the new sewage regulations.[75] They fought back rather than allowing themselves to be forced to leave.

Another strategy was strength in numbers. Not only had most of the Chinese in urban areas physically congregated, by choice and by force, into sections of the cities known as Chinatowns, but in talking about the Overseas Chinese in San Francisco, Roberta Greenwood quotes the sociologist Stanford Lyman, who said, "It was in Chinatown that the lonely Chinese laborer could find fellowship, companions, social familiarity, and solace. Chinatown acted as a partial buffer against the prejudices, hatreds, and depredations of hostile whites."[76] They also formed groups like the Chinese Consolidated Benevolent Association (CCBA). The CCBA was one of the largest organizations, but there were other family or clan associations formed to help any member in need.[77] The Chinese communities "established benevolent or mutual-aid organizations, clan associations, and secret societies with varying degrees of connection to the homeland. Members of clan associations could equally be joined to the district organization, and possibly even hold a position in a prominent secret society all at the same time. Only in certain situations did these cross-ties become apparent."[78]

Since it was not legal for Chinese persons to own property in many American cities by 1887, often they would have a European American agent purchase the land or business and then pay rent to the agent.[79] In other instances, such as in Deadwood, South Dakota, the Chinese community made their existence extremely visible. Albeit a small community, they held their celebrations and even their funerals in full sight of and including the entire town.[80]

The Chinese in Missoula

Christopher Higgins, Frank Worden and David Pattee founded the town of Missoula Mills in 1864. In the beginning it was part of Washington Territory and Idaho Territory before becoming part of Montana Territory.[81] The first Chinese began arriving in Montana in the 1860s, and then with the extension of the Northern Pacific Railroad into the Bitterroot Valley, they came more steadily to Missoula. The U.S. Census lists the population of Chinese in Missoula as 44 in 1870, 149 in 1880, 405 in 1890, 208 in 1900, 73 in 1910, 18 in 1920, 14 in 1930 and 8 in 1940.[82] Often though, census records underestimated the Chinese population, and the Chinese Consolidated Benevolent Association encouraged avoidance of registration and the census in protest of anti-Chinese laws in San Francisco.[83] It was quite probable that this was practiced in other places as well as San Francisco once word got out.

The Chinese were not allowed to live in the nicer areas of Missoula and so resided and kept businesses primarily along Front Street.[84] I find this interesting for two reasons. The first being that Front Street was the main artery in town well into the 1920s, which means the Chinese were not exactly out of sight.[85] Their "Chinatown," however, was situated at the far end of the downtown hub, away from where people would arrive to the Garden City by train. The other reason is because Front Street was also the location of the Missoula Mercantile and the Florence Hotel, one of the finest hotels west of the Mississippi.[86] The intersection of Higgins Avenue and Front Street was the seat of commerce and politics in early Missoula, and the small Chinatown was merely a block away in either direction to the east and west.

According to Sanborn Fire Insurance Maps from 1884 to 1912, while there was a greater conglomeration of Chinese businesses on the 200 block of West Front Street, there were Chinese businesses and dwellings a few blocks to the east and to the north. There were also areas in and around the Missoula city limits where the Chinese were scattered, some on farms and ranches.

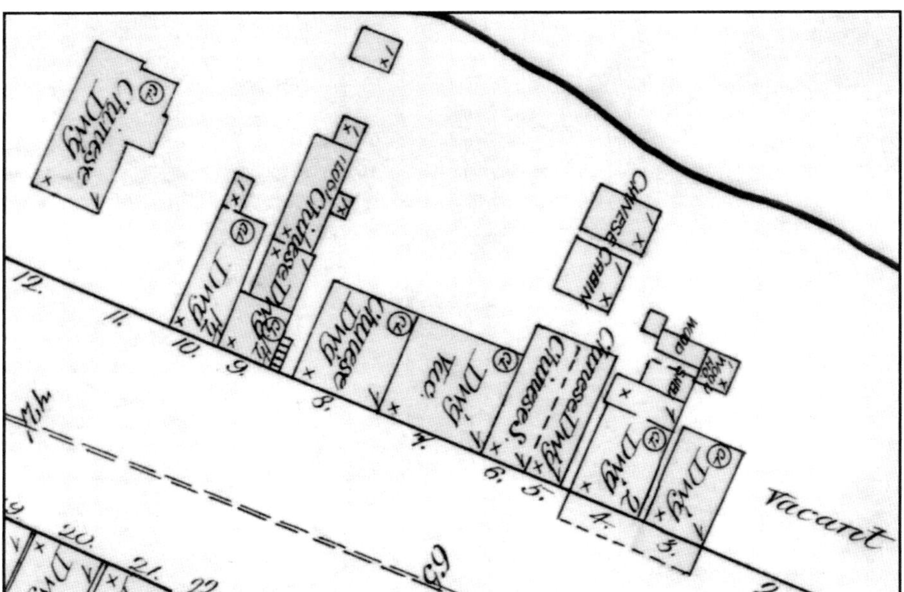

A detail of an 1884 Sanborn Fire Insurance Map for the 200 block of West Front Street, Missoula, depicting the small "Chinatown." *Map used with permission from Environmental Data Resources Inc.*

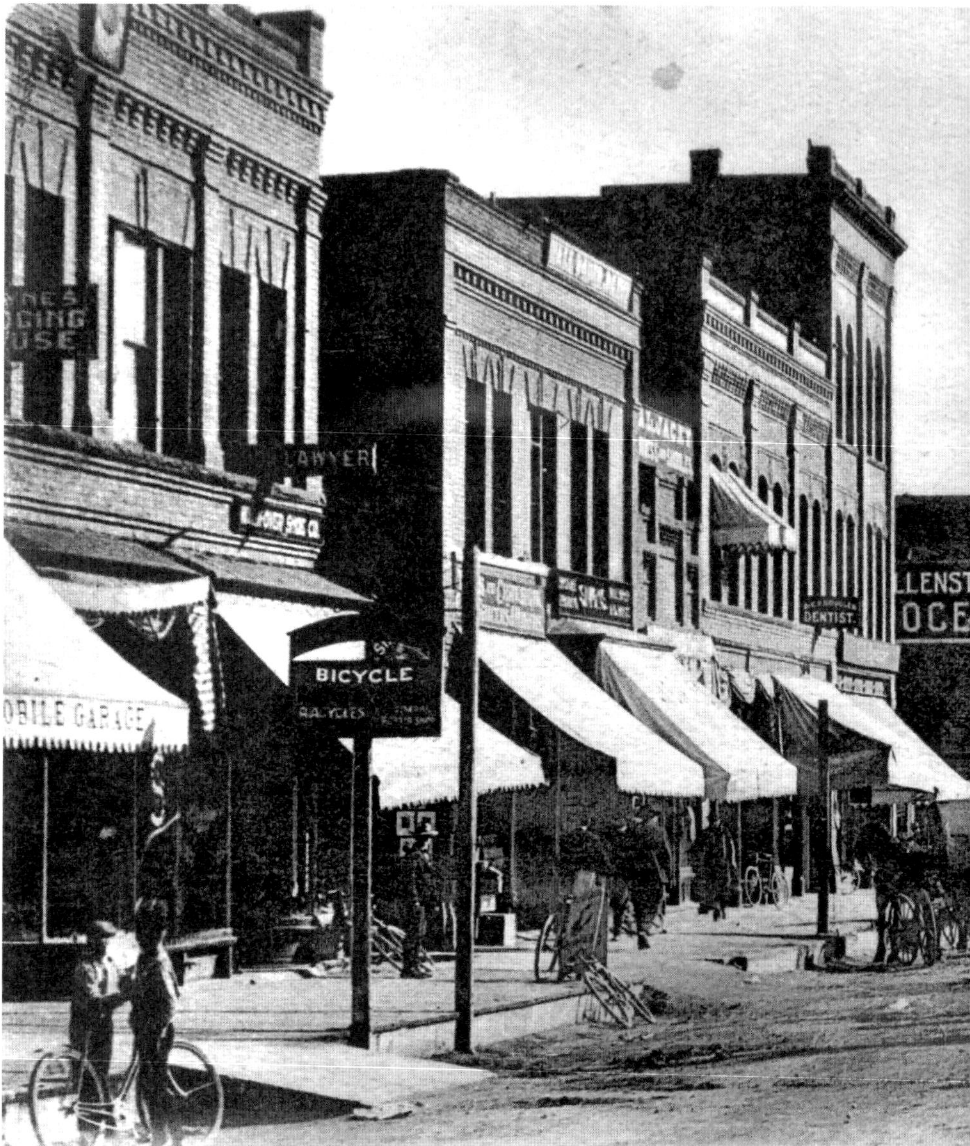

North Higgins Avenue. *Photo No. 74.0154, Archives and Special Collections, Mansfield Library, University of Montana.*

Whether it was due to a small immigrant Chinese population in Missoula or a more tolerant attitude, the anti-Chinese sentiment in Missoula does not appear to have been as hostile as it could be in other places. This did not

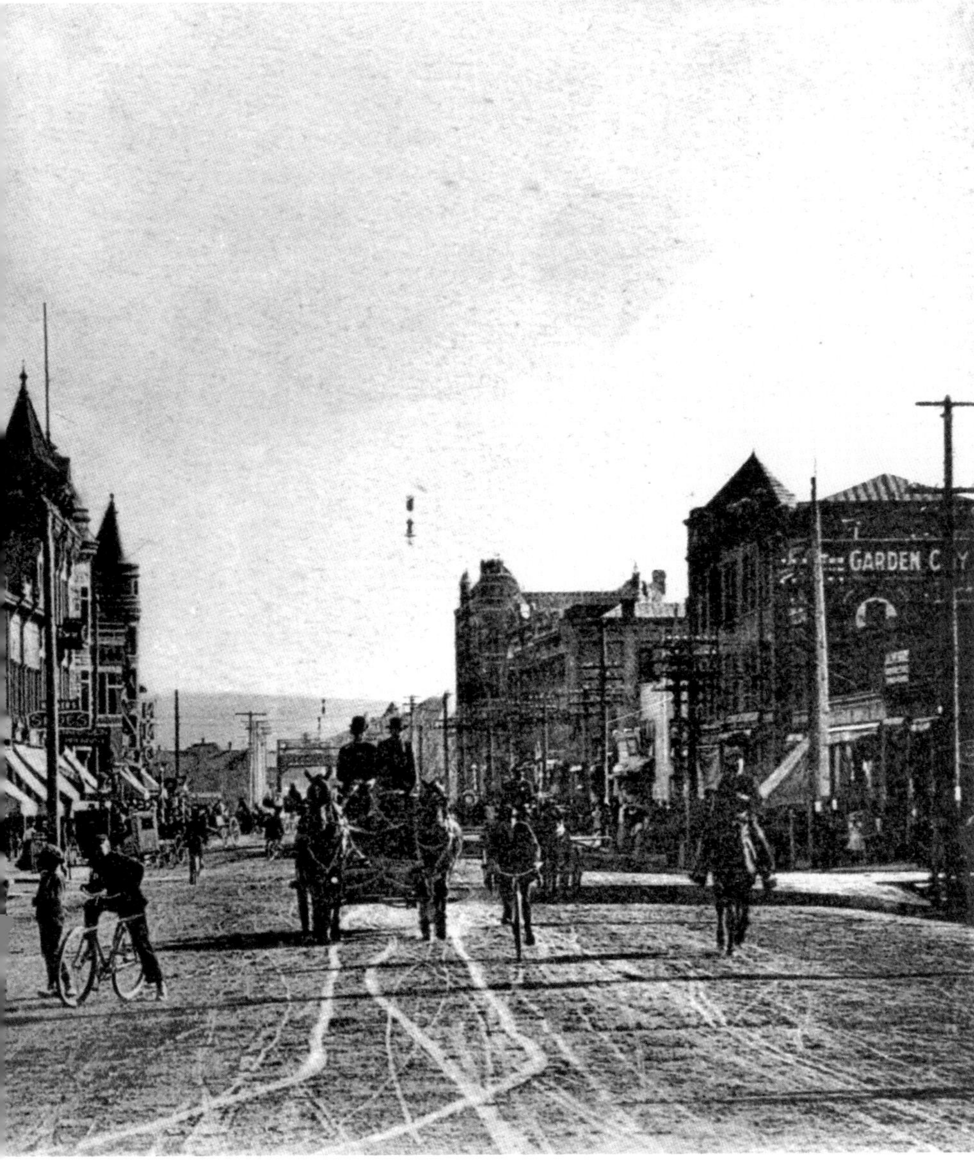

stop Missoulians from using derogatory names such as "celestial," "chink," "almond-eye" and others, but newspaper research shows that authorities were likely to come down on all "tramps, vagrants and suspicious characters," not just the Chinese.[87] Sam Yung, the Chinese restaurateur mentioned earlier in the "respectable" section of West Front Street, appeared to have been a community favorite.[88] Even the "opium king" known as "Cranky Sam" (not to be confused with Sam Yung) was not considered much of a threat every time he was arrested, fined and released.[89]

The 1927 *Missoula Sentinnel* newspaper printed an article reminiscing about Missoula's Chinatown around 1892.[90] It was a favorable article, talking about Chinese festivals, New Years and how they played fantan, a Chinese gambling game, all the time but were hard workers, particularly those who owned laundries. There are a few descriptions of anti-Chinese activity. For example, a group of masked men, all members of the Workingmen's Union, once attacked the ranch of a prosperous Chinese gardener right outside the city limits. One Chinese man was beaten "in a shocking manner" and another "tarred and feathered."[91] The interesting result, however, was that four men were arrested "for complicity in the outrage committed,"[92] suggesting that there was no looking the other way by authorities because the victims were Chinese.

The "Chinese Tunnels"

On March 6, 1900, the Black Plague descended on San Francisco and an immigrant who had recently arrived from China was patient zero. The mayor of that city asked for physician volunteers to complete an inspection of Chinatown (then twelve city blocks) to look for evidence of others stricken with the disease. Dr. William G. Hay was one of the first to volunteer, and his claim was that "he and fellow inspectors had to crawl through an intricate maze of rat holes that connected the houses in an underground network of secret passages" and that relatives would be able to move the sick through these passages "with such neatness and dispatch that no white man can follow them."[93]

It was also assumed by much of the public at the time that if these underground passages and rooms existed, then the San Francisco Chinese must be using them for all forms of vice and vile behavior expected only from the Chinese. However, one author put it this way:

> *All in all, whites who were curious to know what their faithful Chinese houseboy did on his day off would probably have been disappointed. Hours of talk with friends, attendance at a Chinese play or an adult education class sounds dull compared to the exotic pursuits—underground tunnels filled with opium dens and bagnios in which the Chinese were purported to engage.*[94]

In 1897, Frank Norris, an American novelist with a naturalist style of writing, printed a short story called "The Third Circle." The "three circles" were the three parts of San Francisco's Chinatown—at least in his opinion and that of many others. "In reality there are three parts of Chinatown—the part the guides show you, the part the guides don't show you, and the part that no one ever hears of."[95] The story goes on to tell of a couple who went about touring Chinatown without guides, searching for the "authentic Chinatown." The wife is ultimately kidnapped, and although never seen again by her husband, she is discovered twenty years later by the narrator in the story, in the "third circle," strung out on opium, living in an opium den as a prostitute with a different name and no recollection of her life before the kidnapping.[96] This story and ones like it were not uncommon around the turn of the twentieth century.

Even with stories such as this, in the 1880s, there was a rise in tourism in San Francisco as people searched for a different kind of American West. The interest was more in experiences with the "other" that helped them set themselves apart and make sense of the changing society around them and their future place in it. The best place to find this in San Francisco was Chinatown, and of course, shrewd entrepreneurs latched onto the economic possibilities without thought as to the cultural and social implications for Chinese American identity.[97]

In places like San Francisco's Chinatown, tour guides promised the opportunity to glimpse what the "real Chinatown" was like beyond the restaurants, shops and typical tourist traps. When the scenes of opium smoking, gambling and other deprivation became less frequent, threatening their bottom line, the tour guides began to pay Chinatown residents to fake those activities in dark basements and alleys away from the light of day. Recounting W.H. Gleadell's tourist experience written in "Night Scenes in Chinatown," historian Raymond Rast suggests that this is where the entire "Chinese underground" myth began. It was "rumored to be a vast labyrinth of opium dens, gambling halls, criminal hideouts, and slave quarters that extended four or more stories below ground."[98]

Although, Rast also talks about Charles Dobie, a writer and a Chinatown tour guide in the 1890s, who admits in his writing about San Francisco's Chinatown that the labyrinth of tunnels was as fake as the scenes they paid Chinatown residents to reenact and that these underground spaces "grew in legend until practically every stranger…repeated marvelous tales of how it burrowed down five, six, seven, eight stories underground." In reality, tourists were only one story underground, led in a twisted maze of sloping landscape to make them believe they were much lower than they were.[99]

Rumors about Chinese undergrounds also suggest that most of the Chinese lived underground, in basements and strange underground structures. Many times the reason for this was simple: urban sprawl often pushed in on the small Chinatowns, causing them to often live in any affordable space they could find, including basements.[100] They also "had little choice but to subdivide their rooms, dig out basements, and build lofts or tiers of bunks."[101] Bunk beds with a number of layers are sometimes considered to be the sign of a possible opium den, but as it is described here, it was often just a necessity to have many people living under the same roof. To circle back to the Missoula underground project, there are a number of instances where these facts can explain some of the underground spaces. For instance, in the case where bunk beds, opium paraphernalia and Chinese coins were found, the conclusion was made that it must have been an opium den.

4

BASEMENTS, BROTHELS AND... OPIUM DENS?

An ingenious labyrinth contrived out of connecting basements and narrow passageways
—Charles Dobie

The goal of this project was to answer the research question of whether or not an archaeological signature could be found in the Missoula underground to support the stories of "Chinese tunnels" and underground activity by the Chinese. The hypothesis was that if there was a lot of Chinese activity underground, there would be evidence to support this, such as archival documentation (city and building records or photos, for example) or material evidence (remnants of medicinal and/or opium paraphernalia and other "personal and domestic objects") that has become common in the work of Overseas Chinese archaeology.[102] This also would have included the layout of underground space that might suggest Chinese occupation based on architectural features or symbols, exposure and access to the space.[103] Lacking the evidence in this first foray into the Missoula underground does not completely disprove the hypothesis, but it is definitely cause for discussion, further research and offering of alternative explanations.

First, looking at each of the project sites in relation to the existence and use of the units of analysis (basements, sidewalk voids and any type of tunnel or tunnel access) provides telling evidence. The research shows that, ironically, the documented and archaeologically evident use of underground spaces was least at the known Chinese-related sites. At the other sites, there was use of the basements and sidewalk voids for various purposes, and only two

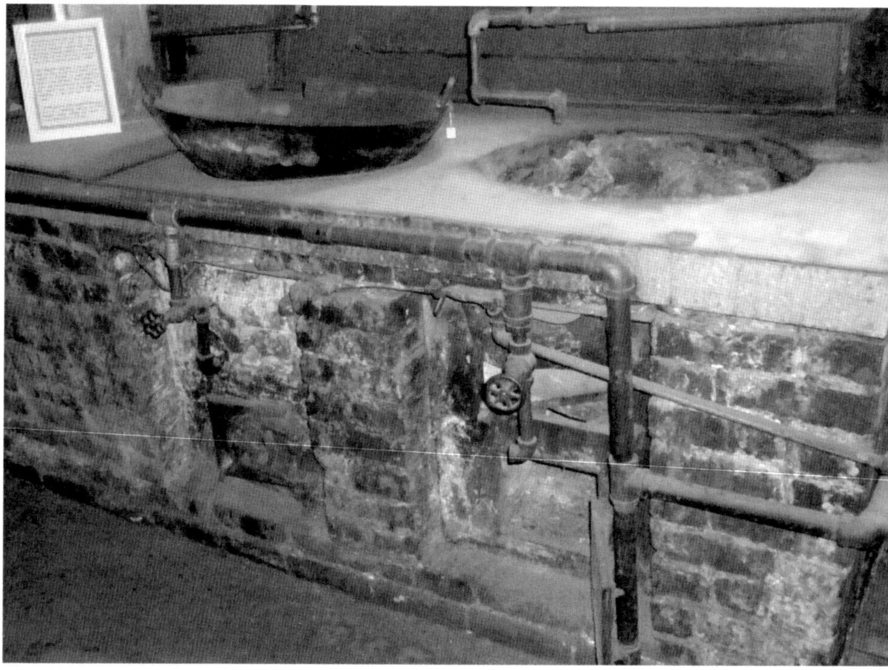

Cooking stove with Chinese wok used at the Mai Wah Noodle Parlor, Butte, Montana. *Author's collection.*

sites connected to the steam tunnel system. There were a number of other properties visited during the project where information was gathered but not fully incorporated into the study. These were all considered in context to the eight project sites, and specific known use was noted.

The historical research shows that the Riverside Café was the location of two Chinese businesses (a restaurant and a store). This is not surprising given that the property was part of the biggest conglomeration of Chinese businesses and dwellings in Missoula at that time. Yet, there is nothing archaeological or architectural to suggest any other use of the basement as told by general oral history. MacKenzie River Pizza Company, which was once Sam Yung's Chinese restaurant for the first half of the twentieth century, has been altered, and the basement, a renovated space with a modern, professional kitchen in it today, has no extant (or apparent) archaeological signatures found at Chinese restaurants elsewhere in the state such as the Mai Wah, Noodles and Chop Suey in Butte, Montana.[104] Except for the historic documentation, it would be impossible today to recognize any archaeological signature of a Chinese business, let alone basement and sidewalk void use by a Chinese business.

The site at the present-day Piece of Mind shop on West Main Street does raise some questions about Chinese underground use. The historical research suggests that the building was not actually a Chinese restaurant, and yet there is Chinese writing on the wall in the basement. The other concerning aspect of the graffiti is the conflicting translations of the writing between the "expert" quoted in the 1958 *Missoulian* article and the recent six who attempted translation during this project. The oral history of Chinese prostitution cribs along this block adds another bit to the mystery, but no actual evidence has been found to prove or disprove such activities. Perhaps this basement was used as a Chinese prostitution crib or perhaps for gambling or as an opium den—the three most common suggested Chinese uses of underground spaces from the oral history. Keeping in mind the need for multiple lines of evidence, the research just does not support the stories. The writing on the wall, however, cannot be overlooked and is worthy of continued research.

Historical archaeologists Kate and Melanie Giles examined the graffiti found in late nineteenth- and early twentieth-century farm buildings in East Yorkshire, England, concluding that the graffiti "were created by a group of young men at the bottom of the social hierarchy."[105] They were young farm boys and hired farm hands with little or no education. This would have been similar to the Chinese population in Missoula at a time when the Chinese were not particularly popular. The striking thing about the Giles study is that the graffiti provided a window into the everyday lives of these boys and a history that would otherwise not be known. In East Yorkshire they were able to compare the graffiti with oral histories. Combined with surveys of the buildings, noting the location of the graffiti in each, they had the multiple lines of evidence that are lacking for the Piece of Mind basement.

The three Chinese associated sites are the only properties on the list that do not have a documented or archaeologically evident underground use. Piece of Mind, however, is noted as being questionable because of the writing and the fact that, although the basement is documented by some secondary sources as once being a Chinese restaurant, primary sources such as Sanborn maps and city records that have been found so far do not support this assertion. Another item to note is the question regarding an opium den for another site not directly part of this project. One oral history stated that items were found in the basement or sidewalk void for this property in the 1970s, which suggested the operation of a Chinese opium den at one time. Reportedly, they found such objects as opium smoking paraphernalia, a bag of Chinese coins and a stacked bunk bed four levels high.[106] Because these artifacts have been lost and no photos are known to exist, this is something that cannot be dismissed but also cannot be taken as fact without corroborating evidence to support the claim.

It is necessary to clarify that in no way is the oral history of the Missoula historic underground being dismissed. Oral history is just as crucial to knowing about and understanding our past as any other line of evidence, including archaeology. However, Paul Shackel wrote about public memory and the search for power, stating that collective memories of a group can often come at the expense of a subordinate group.[107] This is not to say this is the case with Missoula and the myths of a Chinese underground. First of all, the belief and perpetuation of the belief in a "Chinese underground" is not unique to Missoula. Second, selective memory that excludes certain aspects of the past and promotes other parts is unfortunately part of creating heritage.[108] The early days of Missoula, like most other urban areas in the American West, were all about promoting the pioneer spirit, industry, mining, building the railroad and progress. Selective memory about ill treatment of any subordinate group and collective memories that bring with them a sense of nostalgia for an earlier, carefree time that support the notions of nation-building is not surprising.[109] Unfortunately, this often creates identities for certain groups, whether it be a social, economic or ethnic group, that are perpetuated through this process of collective memory.

Collective memory is most simply defined as the memory of a group of people, any group of people who share the same story as a memory. Typically, collective memories are communicative by nature because the stories are passed on from one person to another, specifically from one generation to the next. Collective memory is based on everyday communication and storytelling that is shared within and relates to a group, thereby perpetuating a common past.[110] By this definition, collective memory is very much a part of the process explained above in regard to identity. Collective memory can perpetuate myths and, in this case, myths affect the cultural identity of groups like the Chinese in Missoula. Oral history has created a collective memory of the Missoula underground in which the tunnels were built by the Chinese who also used those tunnels to live and travel around town unseen.

There are a number of simple reasons to explain why there have been no findings of an archaeological signature for underground use by any specific group, such as the Chinese. The sample of underground features examined thus far has already shown that the non-Chinese urban population was just as likely to use the underground spaces for storage, business, saloons, cold storage, etc. In the case of the Missoula Mercantile, the reported use of tunnels to hide from public view was due to celebrity in the case of the "John Wayne" tunnel, as opposed to the urban legend that the Chinese often used tunnels to travel about the city to stay out of public view. So far, and with much more work still to do, it seems that these tunnels, sidewalk voids and basement spaces were built and intended to be part of the overall downtown Missoula infrastructure. In a tight urban environment, the exploitation of marginal spaces served economic and practical purposes and, perhaps secondarily, social and cultural needs as well.

Progress and development of a downtown area must also be considered. Needs change, and the infrastructure and built environment are continuously changing to meet those needs. Many of the buildings have been heavily renovated without basement spaces or other parts of the building being surveyed or recorded. Thus it is useful to consider other aspects of the city that are more about daily life.[111] It is important to look beyond the obvious major buildings and landmarks. Group interaction is intense in an urban environment and inevitably will leave behind some kind of archaeological signature of everyday life, but the key is to narrow in on where and how those interactions occur. Cultural practice and material evidence are incomplete without considering social conditions that altogether show interactions that could point to an archaeology of identity.[112]

Sometimes it is not about the big picture, the major events and well-known people but about the mundane things that make up life in the urban landscape. The physicality of the city can be read "as a text of social and cultural history—especially the history of ordinary, everyday people."[113] While this is true, it is important to avoid a slippery slope into false interpretation. For example, Chinese writing on a basement wall as discussed in Chapter 3 does not automatically equate with the use of the space by Chinese individuals. Without any other evidence to back it up, it is not possible to create a complete cultural history for that building based on the writing.

Over three decades ago, Robert Schuyler asked whether ethnicity is recognizable in the archaeological record.[114] Since then, archaeology in general has been providing alternatives for examining how people construct and maintain identity and how ethnicity is a part of that identity.[115] Just as historical archaeology can help make sense of the complicated interactions in urban settings, so can considering identity as encompassing more than ethnicity, but also social and economic class and gender.

This is not to say that archaeological sites cannot have "ethnic markers" or that they do not exist at all. An assortment of particular artifacts can indeed point to a certain ethnic group, but there must be caution against taking this as an absolute.[116] The law of equifinality applied to archaeology requires vigilance for avoiding sweeping generalizations, understanding and accepting that the possibility exists for multiple explanations of the findings. It only affirms that the archaeological assemblage is not the end answer but suggests the beginning, to know what research questions to ask about the site and why we as archaeologists are asking them. Continuing the research with multiple lines of evidence and incorporating oral history, social history and a knowledgeable understanding of material culture that separates itself from the ideas and traditional academic cultural expectations can force more in-depth and complete analyses.[117]

5

URBAN ARCHAEOLOGY AND FUTURE DIRECTIONS

Urban archaeology continues to produce an increasingly complex vision of material life in cities that unseats many ideological notions of urban life and confronts the complicated social life of urban folk.
—Mullins and Warner[118]

The intention here has never been to myth-bust local lore or to disprove the oral history that connects historic underground spaces to the Overseas Chinese population in the early American West. Even if that had been the goal, it is fair to say that it was not accomplished. There are a number of theories that could be supported with the data collected. What the project has done is produce some concrete facts about the use of Missoula's underground spaces during the dates covered so far, from the founding of Missoula in 1867 to 1920, and has suggested a few explanations for the findings. It is suggested that a more complete picture of historic underground use can be formed by examining closely the Prohibition-era, the history of female boardinghouses and the Cold War–era fallout shelters. Another suggestion is to begin a comparison of other Montana towns that have underground spaces and tunnels to broaden the scope from there to other cities in the American West, the United States and even globally.

Of course, for work like this to even have a future, preservation issues must be addressed, especially in an ever-changing urban environment. The National Historic Preservation Act (NHPA) of 1966 provides the most succinct explanation for why preservation matters:

> *The spirit and direction of the Nation are founded upon and reflected in its historic heritage; the historical and cultural foundations of the Nation should be preserved as a living part of our community life and development in order to give a sense of orientation to the American people.*[119]

One of the key ingredients for understanding historical and cultural heritage is education. In many cases, we get caught up in the legal jargon and laws that regulate preservation. At times, the very same legislation that is supposed to guide preservation actually is used against it in the search for loopholes that allow inadequate effort to be made in protecting heritage. Even in better circumstances, the focus is generally on saving the historic resource first, and then, if that is managed, it becomes a tool for promoting heritage. If we were to think about it the other way around and promote heritage through education and dialogue, preserving the resource starts to make more sense and serves a deeper purpose than "saving another old building."

While it may not be possible to preserve every building, sidewalk void, tunnel and basement or all of the data contained therein, it is realistic to set a standard practice of recording and documenting many of these spaces to understand how people used and adapted to their built environment in urban settings. The most perfect example from the Missoula Historic Underground Project of such activity being valuable is from the Top Hat Bar. Renovations greatly altered the structure inside and out. Without the opportunity of a well-timed archaeological survey prior to those renovations, the existence and documentation of the hidden basement door would have been lost, with no way to systematically connect the location of the door to what was once underground storage.

Again, clearly preserving or even documenting everything is not at all realistic. It is necessary to be selective, and who gets to make those decisions is not always based on the most optimal motivations.[120] Pointing the finger at politics, stronger influence of one group over another, commercialism or simply necessary economic development as the catalysts for heritage preservation decision making is easy. The harder part is finding a viable solution. Ideally, archaeology and other disciplines mentioned earlier could become more integrated with historic preservation programs and urban planning. This could open up opportunities to conduct more surveys such as the Missoula Historic Underground Project that answer many questions about a city's history and by making that history more relevant during discussions of city development.

In an urban environment, different social, political, economic and ethnic group interaction is very intense. Because of this, we can often observe patterns that are a product of these interactions in an archaeological context. Urban archaeology is challenging in many ways but also well situated to study this social group interaction.[121] Historical documentation—maps, property records, assessments and land surveys—contributes to research in historical and urban archaeology and aids in understanding how a town is designed. This also requires the ability to see how "would-be cities worked in the larger cultural landscape of the past."[122] For instance, based on their societal and cultural differences, the Chinese were often settled on the periphery and separated from the mainstream society, a measurable variable in spatial analysis. This in turn greatly affected their access to wealth and status. This stratification has been documented elsewhere in the way space is used "to reinforce and resist relations of power, authority, and inequality."[123] Thus, there is precedence for the complex ways in which differentiation of space can reinforce power and authority, as seen in the practice of pushing the Chinese to the outskirts or even driving them away completely. Space was also used to resist such hostile social settings, as in the creation of Chinatowns and the inaccessible spaces that were not user friendly to the non-Chinese visitor.

Again, context becomes a critical factor. Often in oral and written history there might be those with an agenda when it comes to historical narratives. On the other hand, there can be a tendency to lean to the complete other extreme and draw conclusions that are too broad.[124] Anthropologists are in a unique position to "read" and use all of the evidence available (i.e., geography, cartography, architecture, archaeology, history) to them and offer valuable insight into urban landscape examination, but caution must be taken not to privilege one source over another. For this project, archaeological and archival research, map reading and mapmaking, analysis of architecture—not only of the exterior but also the interior of structures—and spatial analysis of the urban landscape have been key.

Future Directions

Barbara Voss and Rebecca Allen outlined three primary challenges created by current historical archaeology of the Overseas Chinese that should be taken into consideration when determining future directions of a project such as this: localized points of reference, research based on acculturation and Orientalism.[125] All of these challenges were faced during the underground project and will continue to be dealt with as this line of research continues. First, while secondary sources were consulted about the history of underground spaces in other cities, a current survey in those cities has not been conducted. Given the time and scope limitations of the project thus far, it is a reasonable exclusion and does open the possibility for future research in an area that is lacking within urban archaeology. In some cases, the presence of "underground" features may not even be recognized, but using the units of analysis from this project—basement, tunnel, sidewalk void—an extensive study could be conducted to compare the historic use of underground space in multiple urban areas at regional, national and international scales. Looking at sites in isolation instead of in comparison to one another greatly limits what can be learned; thus a broader, comparative study is essential to contextualize interpretations of underground spaces in Missoula and elsewhere.[126]

Second, to prove or disprove the hypothesis, archaeological signatures (i.e., ethnic markers) of a "Chinese underground" and/or evidence of underground use by the Chinese were sought. This makes the cautions by Voss and Allen about acculturation quite relevant here.[127] Couching any historical or archaeological research in terms of how a particular group, such as Chinese immigrants in the American West, integrate into the larger society in which they live leaves us open to overlooking so many other aspects of those human interactions in the intense urban environment. In turn, this dangerously leads to possible false interpretations of cultural identity and possible perpetuation of cultural myths.

Third, Orientalism "can be understood as a Western belief in a radical and essential difference between the East and the West."[128] It was discussed earlier how the origins of a "Chinese tunnel" construct may have developed—primarily with an early American fascination with and beliefs about the Chinese as being vastly different from the rest of the community in which they lived. Granted, differences exist; however, it is not the perspective with which to ask a research question, nor the best terms in which to explain the outcome of that research.

For future work dedicated to this type of urban landscape, it is recommended that more research be conducted about the use of underground spaces without looking for such things as "ethnic markers" at the outset. It is first important to understand the roles that an underground infrastructure played (or plays) in an urban environment in order to search for similarities that are generally consistent with the use of underground space. At that point, it might be possible to find the differences that would produce the richness of data about the process of urbanization and create a context and framework within which to form hypotheses and determine whether ethnicity is even part of that discussion.

AFTERWORD

Many people continue to ask about the future of the Missoula Historic Underground Project (MHUP). It is by no means over, that is for sure. I continue to collect oral histories from people I meet randomly, who are referred to me or who contact me directly and am still conducting archival research. I am still available and willing to look at any basement or sidewalk void or tunnel in the downtown area and beyond. When given the opportunity, documentation of these underground spaces continues as well. Future work will include considering the underground spaces of other cities in Montana (Butte and Havre), Boise, Seattle, Portland and Sacramento to continue the search for the so-called Chinese connection to underground spaces.

I am not alone in this endeavor. There are other students at the University of Montana who are very interested in continuing similar work. As mentioned in this book, I was only able to consider eight properties from the time period of 1860 to 1920. Dylan Kemp, an archaeology student who has been very involved in this project, is interested in looking at the Missoula historic underground from the Prohibition-era perspective, conducting similar research from 1920 through approximately 1940. There is an upcoming collaboration between the data collected thus far, that Prohibition data and a project that graduate student Kelli Casias is working on about bootlegging during Prohibition. Her research focuses primarily on women's moonshining activities in the Montana cities of Anaconda and Butte. This will begin to connect historic underground use in various urban areas to form a broader picture in scope and time.

Afterword

Thank you for reading this book and for attending all of the events that have been and will be associated with the Missoula historic underground. I am often asked whether there will be an underground tour in Missoula someday like the ones in Butte, Havre, Seattle, Portland and so on, and I believe that would be a very worthwhile endeavor in the future. I suppose the best answer I have for that is…stay tuned!

I feel very blessed having the opportunity to be such a big part of an amazing project—one that is integral to Missoula's history and cultural heritage. The entire community has been so patient, supportive and interested for the past two and a half years, and I hope that partnership continues for years to come. If you want or have more information, photos, stories or anything (including letting me know I got something wrong!) that will increase the knowledge base of the Missoula Historic Underground Project, please contact me at manning.nikkm@gmail.com. You can also stay involved through the project Facebook page, www.facebook.com/missoulahistoricundergroundproject.

NOTES

Preface

1. Philip Maechling, personal communication with the author, 2012.

Introduction

2. Schara, "HABS Guidelines."
3. Barth, *Ethnic Groups and Boundaries*; Tung, *Chinese in America*; Wegars, *Hidden Heritage*; Pan, *Encyclopedia of the Chinese Overseas*; Ahmad, *Opium Debate*; Pfaelzer, *Driven Out.*
4. Lai, *Forbidden City*; May, *Historic Pendleton*; Lee, Lim and Matsukawa, *Re/Collecting Early Asian America*; Schablitsky, *Box Office Archaeology*; Speidel, *Sons of the Profits.*
5. Ramenofsky and Steffen, *Unit Issues in Archaeology*.
6. *Basement Encroachment and Sidewalk Obstruction Study, Missoula Central Business District.*
7. Doug Harbey, personal communication with the author, 2012.

Chapter 1

8. Nee and Nee, *Longtime Californ'*, 71.
9. Lai, *Forbidden City*, 6.
10. "Portland Underground FAQ."
11. May, *Historic Pendleton*.
12. Speidel, *Sons of the Profits*, 214.
13. Kathryn McAlpin, personal communication with the author.
14. *Chicago Daily Tribune*, January 26, 1858; *Chicago Daily Press and Tribune*, October 4, 1858; *Chicago Daily Press and Tribune*, January 1, 1859; *The Press and Tribune*, May 5, 1859.
15. Turdo, *Nazareth's Underground*, 4.
16. Ibid., 29.
17. Grimm et al., "Integrated Approaches," 571–84.
18. Low, "Anthropology of Cities," 384.
19. Ingold, "Temporality of the Landscape," 152.
20. Church, "Grant and the Grid," 220.
21. See Mrozowski, "Epilogue," 135–36, for further discussion of collaboration in archaeology.
22. *Basement Encroachment and Sidewalk Obstruction Study*.
23. Smith, "Landscape Representation," 71–88.
24. Ibid., 73.
25. Ibid., 83.
26. Valentino, "Using Maps," 40–41.
27. Staski, "Living in Cities Today," 6.
28. Morriss, *Archaeology of Buildings*, 14.
29. *Basement Encroachment and Sidewalk Obstruction Study*.
30. Delle, "Landscapes of Class Negotiation," 137.

Chapter 2

31. Greenwood, *Down by the Station*, 41.
32. Orser, *Historical Archaeology*, 251.
33. Ibid., 252.
34. *Polk's Missoula City Directory*.

35. *Basement Encroachment and Sidewalk Obstruction Study*, D10–12, D37.
36. John Coffee, personal communication with the author, 2012.
37. "Montana Historical and Architectural Inventory."
38. *Basement Encroachment and Sidewalk Obstruction Study*, C5, D40.
39. Nicole Garr, personal communication with the author, 2012.
40. See Lai, *Forbidden City*, for a discussion regarding the misspelling of Chinese names in city, court, tax and property records.
41. *Helena Independent*, "Four Men Arrested," August 25, 1891; *Washington Post*, "Driving the Chinese from Missoula," August 25, 1891; Alexander Saxton, *Indispensable Enemy*; Gyory, *Closing the Gate*; Baxter, "Response of California's Chinese," 29–36.
42. Ahmad, *Opium Debate*, 28.
43. *Basement Encroachment and Sidewalk Obstruction Study*, D33.
44. Missoula Fire Department Scrapbook, Collection MSS 507, Archives and Special Collections, Mansfield Library, University of Montana.
45. Curl, *Dictionary of Architecture*, 37; Rabun, *Structural Analysis*, 72.
46. *Basement Encroachment and Sidewalk Obstruction Study*, C6.
47. Pei-Lin Yu, personal communication with the author, 2014.
48. Don Millhouse, personal communication with the author, 2014.
49. Jeff MacDonald, personal communication with the author, 2013.
50. *Basement Encroachment and Sidewalk Obstruction Study*, C6, D45.
51. Philip Maechling, personal communication with the author, 2012.
52. Missoula Fire Department Scrapbook, Collection MSS 507, Archives and Special Collections, Mansfield Library, University of Montana.
53. Smith, *Missoula Mercantile*.
54. Philip Maechling, personal communication with the author, 2012; Ty Robinson, personal communication with the author, 2014.
55. Jed Dennison, personal communication with the author, 2012.
56. Jeff MacDonald, personal communication with the author, 2013.
57. Scott Loken and Solomon Martin, personal communication with the author, 2013.
58. *Basement Encroachment and Sidewalk Obstruction Study*, D42–43.
59. Kirk and Bauer, *History of the Montana Power Company*, 174.
60. Koelbel, *Missoula*, 60.
61. Johnson, "Andrew B. Hammond," 154.

Chapter 3

62. Voss and Allen, "Overseas Chinese Archaeology," 10.
63. Barth, *Bitter Strength*; Voss and Allen, "Overseas Chinese Archaeology"; Merritt, "Coming Man From Canton"; Seonnichsen, *Chinese Exclusion Act*.
64. Takaki, *Strangers from a Different Shore*, 85.
65. Voss and Allen, "Overseas Chinese Archaeology," 11.
66. Cassel, *Chinese in America*; Chen, *Being Chinese*.
67. Baxter, "Response of California's Chinese," 30.
68. Dicker, *Chinese in San Francisco*, 13.
69. Rast, "Cultural Politics of Tourism," 58.
70. Chen, *Chinese San Francisco*, 81–82.
71. Costello et al., "Luck of Third Street," 136, 148.
72. Dicker, *Chinese in San Francisco*, 18; Ahmad, *Opium Debate*.
73. Baxter, "Response of California's Chinese," 29; Hoobler and Hoobler, *Chinese American Family Album*, 63–64.
74. Baxter, "Response of California's Chinese," 29.
75. Cassel, *Chinese in America*.
76. Greenwood, "Overseas Chinese at Home," 43.
77. Hoobler and Hoobler, *Chinese American Family Album*, 82.
78. Merritt, "Coming Man from Canton," 248–49.
79. Baxter, "Response of California's Chinese," 33.
80. Fosha and Leatherman, "Chinese Experience in Deadwood," 99.
81. Smith, *Missoula Mercantile*, 14.
82. Koelbel, *Missoula*, 59–60.
83. Swartout and Fritz, *Montana Heritage*, 65; Baxter, "Response of California's Chinese," 31.
84. Koelbel, *Missoula*, 59.
85. Mathews, *Montana Mainstreets*; Smith, *Missoula Mercantile*.
86. Mathews, *Montana Mainstreets*.
87. *Weekly Missoulian*, "Police Are Cleaning the City of Undesirables," June 28, 1908.
88. *Daily Missoulian*, "Sam Yung at Work," March 31, 1912.
89. *Weekly Missoulian*, "Opium King Spends Night in Jail," June 24, 1908.
90. *Missoula Sentinnel*, "Chinatown—Missoula Had One Back in 1892," November 7, 1927.
91. *Washington Post*, "Driving the Chinese from Missoula," August 25, 1891.
92. *Helena Independent*, "Four Men Arrested," August 25, 1891.
93. Kalisch, "Black Death in Chinatown," 119.

94. Dicker, *Chinese in San Francisco*, 19.
95. Rast, "Cultural Politics of Tourism," 29.
96. Ibid., 30.
97. Ibid., 29–43.
98. Ibid., 46. For more Chinatown tourist accounts and descriptions of the scenery in which they found themselves, see: Gleadell, "Night Scenes in Chinatown," 378–383; Carey, *By the Golden Gate*; Asbury, *Barbary Coast*; Genthe, *As I Remember*; Buel, *Sunlight and Shadow*.
99. Dobie and Suydam, *San Francisco's Chinatown*; Rast, "Cultural Politics of Tourism," 47, 120.
100. Yip, "Association, Residence, and Shop," 109–17.
101. Rast, "Cultural Politics of Tourism," 34.

Chapter 4

102. Wegars, "Asian American Comparative Collection," 166.
103. Yip, "Association, Residence, and Shop."
104. "Mai Wah Society."
105. Giles and Giles, "Writing on the Wall," 336–57.
106. Darrell Johnson, personal communication with the author, 2014.
107. Shackel, "Public Memory," 655–70.
108. Ibid., 655–62.
109. Ibid., 655.
110. Assmann and Czaplicka, "Collective Memory," 125–33.
111. Blackmar, "Urban Landscape," 12–14.
112. Jones, *Archaeology of Ethnicity*, 128.
113. Groth, "Generic Buildings," 41–44.
114. Schuyler, *Archaeological Perspectives*.
115. Banks, *Ethnicity*; Dixon, *Boomtown Saloons*; Nagel, "Constructing Ethnicity," 152–76; Franklin and Fesler, *Historical Archaeology*; Orser, *Race and the Archaeology of Identity*; Orser, *Archaeology of Race and Racialization*; Scott, *Those of Little Note*; Orser, "Challenge of Race," 661–68.
116. Praetzellis and Praetzellis, "Mangling Symbols of Gentility," 645–54; Wegars, "Who's Been Workin' on the Railroad?," 37–65.
117. Mullins, "Strange and Unusual," 152–57; Voss, "Archaeology of Overseas Chinese Communities," 424–39.

Chapter 5

118. Mullins and Warner, "Introduction," 2.
119. National Historic Preservation Act (16 U.S.C. 470 et seq.).
120. Lozny, *Landscapes Under Pressure*, 16.
121. Staski, "Living in Cities Today," 5–8.
122. Purser and Shaver, "Plats and Place," 27.
123. Rotman and Nassaney, "Class, Gender, and the Built Environment," 42.
124. Church, "Grant and the Grid," 222.
125. Voss and Allen, "Overseas Chinese Archaeology."
126. Delle, "Landscapes of Class Negotiation," 136, 154.
127. Voss and Allen, "Overseas Chinese Archaeology," 19.
128. Ibid.

BIBLIOGRAPHY

Adams, William Hampton. "Review of Models of Spatial Inequality: Settlement Patterns in Historical Archaeology by Robert Paynter." *Historical Archaeology* 19 (1985): 135–36.

Ahmad, Diana L. *The Opium Debate and Chinese Exclusion Laws in the Nineteenth-Century American West*. Reno: University of Nevada Press, 2007.

Anschuetz, Kurt F., Richard H. Wilshusen and Cherie L. Scheick. "An Archaeology of Landscapes: Perspectives and Directions." *Journal of Archaeological Research* 9 (2001): 157–211.

Arnold, J. Barto, III, and Sara J. Keyes. "Remembering the 'Queen City of the West': The Untapped Archaeological Resources of Indianola, Texas." *International Journal of Historical Archaeology* 4 (2000): 335–48.

Asbury, Herbert. *The Barbary Coast: An Informal History of the San Francisco Underworld*. New York: Garden City Publishing Company, 1933.

Assmann, Jan, and John Czaplicka. "Collective Memory and Cultural Identity." *New German Critique* 65 (1995): 125–133.

Banks, Marcus. *Ethnicity: Anthropological Constructions*. New York: Psychology Press, 1996.

Barth, Gunther. *Bitter Strength: A History of the Chinese in the U.S., 1850–1870*. Cambridge, MA: Harvard University Press, 1964.

———. *Ethnic Groups and Boundaries*. Cambridge, MA: Harvard University Press, 1964.

Basement Encroachment and Sidewalk Obstruction Study, Missoula Central Business District. Missoula, MT: Dan Sullivan Associates, 1981.

Baxter, R. Scott. "The Response of California's Chinese Populations to the Anti-Chinese Movement." *Historical Archaeology* 42 (2008): 29–36.

Binford, Lewis R. "A Consideration of Archaeological Research Design." *American Antiquity* 29 (1964): 425–41.

Blackmar, Elizabeth. "The Urban Landscape." *Journal of Architectural Education* 30 (1976): 12–14.

Buel, James William. *Sunlight and Shadow of America's Great Cities*. Philadelphia: West Philadelphia Publishing Company, 2010.

Carey, Joseph. *By the Golden Gate; Or, San Francisco, the Queen City of the Pacific Coast: With Scenes and Incidents Characteristic of Its Life*. San Francisco: Albany Diocesan Press, 1902.

Casella, Eleanor C., and James Symonds. *Industrial Archaeology: Future Directions*. New York: Springer, 2005.

Cassel, Susie Lan. *The Chinese in America: A History from Gold Mountain to the New Millennium*. Lanham, MD: AltaMira Press, 2002.

Chen, Shehong. *Being Chinese, Becoming Chinese American*. Chicago: University of Illinois Press, 2002.

Chen, Yong. *Chinese San Francisco, 1850–1943: A Trans-Pacific Community*. Redwood City, CA: Stanford University Press, 2000.

Church, Minette C. "The Grant and the Grid." *Journal of Social Archaeology* 2 (2002): 220–44.

Costello, Julia G., Kevin Hallaran, Keith Warren and Margie Akin. "The Luck of Third Street: Archaeology of Chinatown, San Bernardino, California." *Historical Archaeology* 42 (2008): 136–51.

Curl, James Stevens. *A Dictionary of Architecture and Landscape Architecture*. London: Oxford University Press, 2006.

Delgado, James P. *Gold Rush Port: The Maritime Archaeology of San Francisco's Waterfront*. Oakland: University of California Press, 2009.

Delle, James A. "The Landscapes of Class Negotiation on Coffee Plantations in the Blue Mountains of Jamaica: 1790–1850." *Historical Archaeology* 33 (1999): 136–58.

Dickens, Roy S. *Archaeology of Urban America: The Search for Pattern and Process*. New York: Academic Press, 1982.

Dicker, Laverne Mau. *The Chinese in San Francisco: A Pictorial History*. Mineola, NY: Dover Publications, 1979.

Dixon, Kelly J. *Boomtown Saloons: Archaeology and History in Virginia City*. Reno: University of Nevada Press, 2005.

Dobie, Charles Caldwell, and Edward Howard Suydam. *San Francisco's Chinatown*. New York: Appleton-Century Company, 1936.

Fosha, Rose Estep, and Christopher Leatherman. "The Chinese Experience in Deadwood, South Dakota." *Historical Archaeology* 42 (2008): 97–110.

Franklin, Maria, and Garrett Fesler. *Historical Archaeology, Identity Formation, and the Interpretation of Ethnicity*. Williamsburg, VA: Colonial Williamsburg Foundation, 1999.

Genthe, Arnold. *As I Remember*. New York: Reynal & Hitchcock, 1936.

Giles, Kate, and Melanie Giles. "The Writing on the Wall: The Concealed Communities of the East Yorkshire Horselads." *International Journal of Historical Archaeology* 11 (2007): 336–57.

Gleadell, W.H. "Night Scenes in Chinatown." *The Eclectic Magazine* (1895): 378–83.

Greenwood, Roberta S. *Down by the Station: Los Angeles Chinatown, 1880–1933*. Los Angeles: Institute of Archaeology, University of California, 1978.

———. "The Overseas Chinese at Home: Life in a Nineteenth-Century Chinatown in California." *Archaeology* 31 (1978): 73–86.

Grimm, Nancy B., J. Morgan Grove, Steward T.A. Pickett and Charles L. Redman. "Integrated Approaches to Long-Term Studies of Urban Ecological Systems." *BioScience* 50 (2000): 571–84.

Groth, Paul. "Generic Buildings and Cultural Landscapes as Sources of Urban History." *Journal of Architectural Education* 41 (1988): 41–44.

Gyory, Andrew. *Closing the Gate: Race, Politics, and the Chinese Exclusion Act*. Chapel Hill: University of North Carolina Press, 1998.

Hagaman, Wallace R. *The Chinese Must Go!: The Anti-Chinese Boycott, Truckee, California—1886*. Oakland, CA: Cowboy Press, 2004.

Hoobler, Dorothy, and Thomas Hoobler. *The Chinese American Family Album*. London: Oxford University Press, 1998.

Ingold, Tim. "The Temporality of the Landscape." *World Archaeology* 25 (1993): 152–74.

Johnson, D.L. "Andrew B. Hammond: Education of a Capitalist on the Montana Frontier." PhD diss., University of Montana, 1976.

Jones, Siân. The *Archaeology of Ethnicity: Constructing Identities in the Past and Present*. New York: Psychology Press, 1997.

Kalisch, Philip A. "The Black Death in Chinatown: Plague and Politics in San Francisco 1900–1904." *Arizona and the West* 14 (1972): 113–36.

Kealhofer, Lisa. "Creating Social Identity in the Landscape: Tidewater, Virginia, 1600–1750." In *Archaeologies of Landscape—Contemporary Perspectives*. Edited by Wendy Ashmore and A. Bernard Knapp. London: Blackwell Publishing, 1999, 58–82.

Kirk, Cecil H., and Anne Bauer. *A History of the Montana Power Company*. Pleasant Hill, CA: Donn B. Kirk, 2008.

Koelbel, Lenora. *Missoula: The Way It Was*. Missoula, MT: Gateway Printing, 1979.

Lai, Chuen-Yan David. *The Forbidden City Within Victoria*. Victoria, BC: Orca Book Publishers, 1991.

La Roche, Cheryl J., and Michael L. Blakey. "Seizing Intellectual Power: The Dialogue at the New York African Burial Ground." *Historical Archaeology* 31 (1997): 84–106.

Lee, Erika. *At America's Gates: Chinese Immigration during the Exclusion Era, 1882–1943*. Chapel Hill: University of North Carolina Press, 2004.

Lee, Josephine D., Imogene L. Lim and Yuko Matsukawa. *Re/Collecting Early Asian America: Essays in Cultural History*. Philadelphia: Temple University Press, 2002.

Low, Setha M. "The Anthropology of Cities: Imagining and Theorizing the City." *Annual Review of Anthropology* 25 (1996): 383–409.

Lozny, Ludomir R. *Landscapes Under Pressure: Theory and Practice of Cultural Heritage Research and Preservation*. New York: Springer Publishing, 2006.

"Mai Wah Society: Wah Chong Tai and Mai Wah Noodle Parlor." Mai Wah Historical Society. http://www.maiwah.org/buildings.shtml (accessed May 12, 2014).

Malloy, Maureen. "Introduction." In *Archaeologists and Local Communities: Partners in Exploring the Past*. Edited by Linda Derry and Maureen Malloy. Washington, D.C.: Society for American Archaeology, 2003, ix–xiii.

Mathews, Allan. *Montana Mainstreets*. Vol. 6, *A Guide to Historic Missoula*. Helena: Montana Historical Society, 2003.

May, Keith F. *A Field Guide to Historic Pendleton*. Pendleton, OR: Drigh Sighed Publications, 1997.

Mayne, Alan, and Tim Murray. *The Archaeology of Urban Landscapes: Explorations in Slumland*. New York: Cambridge University Press, 2001.

McBurney, Donald H., and Theresa L. White. *Research Methods*. 7th ed. Belmont, CA: Thomson Wadsworth Publishing, 2007.

McClain, Charles. "Of Medicine, Race, and American Law: The Bubonic Plague Outbreak of 1900." *Law & Social Inquiry* 13 (1998): 447–513.

McDonald, James Robert, and Gary D. Williams. *Missoula Historical Resource Survey*. Missoula, MT: Historical Research Associates, 1980.

Merritt, Christopher. "The Coming Man from Canton: Chinese Experience in Montana 1862–1943." PhD diss., University of Montana, 2010.

Merritt, Christopher W., Gary Weisz and Kelly J. Dixon. "Verily the Road Was Built with Chinaman's Bones: An Archaeology of Chinese Line

Camps in Montana." *International Journal of Historical Archaeology* 16 (2012): 666–95.

"Montana Historical and Architectural Inventory of 134 West Front Street." Missoula Office of Planning and Grants, 2005.

Morriss, Richard K. *The Archaeology of Buildings*. Charleston, SC: Arcadia Publishing, 2000.

Mrozowski, Stephen A. *The Archaeology of Class in Urban America*. New York: Cambridge University Press, 2006.

———. "Epilogue: An Historical Anthropology of American Cities." *Historical Archaeology* 42 (2008): 133–37.

Mullins, Paul R. "The Strange and Unusual: Material and Social Dimensions of Chinese Identity." *Historical Archaeology* 42 (2008): 152–57.

Mullins, Paul R., and Mark S. Warner. "Introduction: Revisiting Living in Cities." *Historical Archaeology* 42 (2008): 1–4.

Murphey, Rhoads. "Boston's Chinatown." *Economic Geography* 28 (1952): 244–55.

Nagel, Joane. "Constructing Ethnicity: Creating and Recreating Ethnic Identity and Culture." *Social Problems* 41 (1994): 152–76.

Nee, Victor, and Brett de Bary Nee. *Longtime Californ': A Documentary Study of an American Chinatown*. San Francisco: Stanford University Press, 1973.

Orser, Charles E., Jr. *The Archaeology of Race and Racialization in Historic America*. Gainesville: University Press of Florida, 2007.

———. "The Challenge of Race to American Historical Archaeology." *American Anthropologist* 100 (1998): 661–68.

———. *Historical Archaeology*. Upper Saddle River, NJ: Pearson Prentice Hall, 2004.

———. *Race and the Archaeology of Identity*. Salt Lake City: University of Utah Press, 2001.

Pan, Lynn. *The Encyclopedia of the Chinese Overseas*. Cambridge, MA: Harvard University Press, 1998.

Pauls, Elizabeth P. "The Place of Space: Architecture, Landscape, and Social Life." In *Historical Archaeology*. Edited by Martin Hall and Stephen W. Silliman. London: Wiley-Blackwell, 2006, 65–83.

Paynter, Robert. *Models of Spatial Inequality: Settlement Patterns in Historical Archeology*. Waltham, MA: Academic Press, 1982.

Pfaelzer, Jean. *Driven Out: The Forgotten War Against Chinese Americans*. Berkeley: University of California Press, 2008.

Pickett, Steward T.A., Mary L. Cadenasso, J. Morgan Grove, Peter M. Groffman, Lawrence E. Band, Christopher G. Boone, William R. Burch Jr., et al. "Beyond Urban Legends: An Emerging Framework of Urban Ecology, as Illustrated by the Baltimore Ecosystem Study." *BioScience* 58 (2008): 139–50.

Polk's Missoula City Directory. N.p.: R.L. Polk and Company, 1903.

"Portland Underground FAQ." Cascade Geographic Society. http://www.shanghaitunnels.info (accessed May 5, 2014).

Praetzellis, Adrian, and Mary Praetzellis. "Mangling Symbols of Gentility in the Wild West: Case Studies in Interpretive Archaeology." *American Anthropologist* 103 (2001): 645–54.

Purser, Margaret, and Noelle Shaver, "Plats and Place: The Transformation of 19th Century Speculation Townsites on the Sacramento River." *Historical Archaeology* 42 (2008): 26–46.

Rabun, J. Stanley. *Structural Analysis of Historic Buildings: Restoration, Preservation, and Adaptive Reuse Applications for Architects and Engineers*. Hoboken, NJ: John Wiley and Sons, 2000.

Ramenofsky, Ann Felice, and Anastasia Steffen. *Unit Issues in Archaeology: Measuring Time, Space, and Material*. Salt Lake City: University of Utah Press, 1998.

Rast, Raymond W. "The Cultural Politics of Tourism in San Francisco's Chinatown, 1882–1917." *Pacific Historical Review* 76 (2007): 29–60.

Redman, Charles L. "Human Dimensions of Ecosystem Studies." *Ecosystems* 2 (1999): 296–98.

Rotman, Deborah L., and Michael S. Nassaney. "Class, Gender, and the Built Environment: Deriving Social Relations from Cultural Landscapes in Southwest Michigan." *Historical Archaeology* 31 (1997): 42–62.

Rotman, Deborah L., and R. Berle Clay. "Urban Archaeology at the Site of the Argosy Casino: The Materiality of Social Change in the Canal Town of Lawrenceburg, Southern Indiana." *Historical Archaeology* 42 (2008): 47–69.

Saxton, Alexander. *The Indispensable Enemy: Labor and the Anti-Chinese Movement in California*. Oakland: University of California Press, 1971.

Schablitsky, Julie M. *Box Office Archaeology: Refining Hollywood's Portrayals of the Past*. Walnut Creek, CA: Left Coast Press, 2012.

Schara, Mark. "HABS Guidelines: Recording Historic Structures and Sites with HABS Measured Drawings." United States Department of the Interior, December 2008.

Schuyler, Robert L. *Archaeological Perspectives on Ethnicity in America: Afro-American and Asian American Culture History*. Amityville, NY: Baywood Publishing Company, 1980.

Scott, Elizabeth M. *Those of Little Note: Gender, Race, and Class in Historical Archaeology*. Tucson: University of Arizona Press, 1994.

Seonnichsen, John. *The Chinese Exclusion Act of 1882*. Santa Barbara, CA: ABC-CLIO/Greenwood, 2011.

Shackel, Paul A. "Public Memory and the Search for Power in American Historical Archaeology." *American Anthropologist* 103 (2001): 655–70.

Smith, Angele. "Landscape Representation: Place and Identity in Nineteenth-Century Ordinance Survey Maps of Ireland." In *Landscape, Memory and History: Anthropological Perspectives*. Edited by Pamela J. Stewart and Andrew Strathern. London: Pluto Press, 2003, 71–88.

Smith, Minie. *The Missoula Mercantile: The Store that Ran an Empire*. Charleston: The History Press, 2012.

Speidel, William. *Sons of the Profits*. Seattle, WA: Nettle Creek Publishing, 1967.

Staski, Edward. "Living in Cities Today." *Historical Archaeology* 42 (2008): 5–10.

Swartout, Robert R., and Harry W. Fritz. *The Montana Heritage: An Anthology of Historical Essays*. Helena: Montana Historical Society Press, 1992.

Swett, Ira L. *Montana's Trolleys*. Vol 3. *Billings, Bozeman, Great Falls, Missoula, Proposed Lines, the Milwaukee Road*. Great Falls, MT: Interurbans Magazine Press, 1970.

Takaki, Ronald. *Strangers from a Different Shore: A History of Asian Americans*. Sudbury, MA: eBookIt.com, 2012.

Tung, William L. *The Chinese in America, 1820–1973: A Chronology & Fact Book*. New York: Oceana Publications, 1974.

Turdo, Mark A. *Nazareth's Underground: A Search Through the Passages of Time*. Nazareth, PA: Moravian Historical Society, 2003.

Valentino, Alicia B. "Using Maps to Aid Our Understanding of a Site's History." *Journal for the Society for Industrial Archaeology* 35 (2009): 39–48.

Voss, Barbara L. "The Archaeology of Overseas Chinese Communities." *World Archaeology* 37 (2005): 424–39.

———. "Between the Household and the World System: Social Collectivity and Community Agency in Overseas Chinese Archaeology." *Historical Archaeology* 42 (2008): 37–52.

———. "Market Street Chinatown Archaeological Project: 2008–2011 Progress Report." San Jose, CA: Stanford University, 2011.

Voss, Barbara L., and Rebecca Allen. "Overseas Chinese Archaeology: Historical Foundations, Current Reflections, and New Directions." *Historical Archaeology* 42 (2008): 5–28.

Wegars, Priscilla. "The Asian American Comparative Collection: A Unique Resource for Archaeologists and Historians." *Historical Archaeology* 42 (2008): 166–70.

———. *Hidden Heritage: Historical Archaeology of the Overseas Chinese*. Amityville, NY: Baywood Publishing Company, 1993.

———. "Who's Been Workin' on the Railroad?: An Examination of the Construction, Distribution, and Ethnic Origins of Domed Rock Ovens on Railroad-Related Sites." *Historical Archaeology* 25 (1991): 37–65.

Yamin, Rebecca. *Digging in the City of Brotherly Love: Stories from Philadelphia Archaeology*. New Haven, CT: Yale University Press, 2008.

Yip, Christopher L. "Association, Residence, and Shop: An Appropriation of Commercial Blocks in North American Chinatowns." *Perspectives in Vernacular Architecture* 5 (1995): 109–17.

Zesch, Scott. "Chinese Los Angeles in 1870–1871: The Makings of a Massacre." *Southern California Quarterly* 90 (2008): 109–58.

INDEX

ABOUT THE AUTHOR

Nikki Manning earned her bachelor's degree in sociology (with a minor in anthropology) at Boston University in Boston, Massachusetts. After a time in the corporate world working in human resources and marketing, she returned to graduate school in the fall of 2011 at the University of Montana and completed a master's degree in anthropology with a concentration in cultural heritage and urban archaeology. Her thesis research focused on the Missoula Historic Underground and explored how the political and social climate of early Missoula may have affected the use of space and the built environment.

Nikki serves on the boards of Preserve Historic Missoula and the Missoula Historic Preservation Commission. She focuses a lot of her energy on historic preservation education and public archaeology. Future goals include earning her PhD in anthropology and continuing research of historic undergrounds and use of urban spaces.

Visit us at
www.historypress.net

This title is also available as an e-book